PERSEVERE

SOLUTIONS FOR PROBLEMS OF INDIVIDUALS, AMERICA, AND THE WORLD

Other Books by the Author

Count the Days

This Far by Faith

As You Think, You Can

Religious Liberty and Last-Day Events

Politics and Religion

The One Book

The Great Controversy and the End

Make Someone Happy

Sunday Lies and Sunday Laws

Jesus: Lord of the Last Days

The Blood-stained Cross and Our Savior

Blessings Through the Times of Trouble

Christ Has a Job for You

PERSEVERE

SOLUTIONS FOR PROBLEMS OF INDIVIDUALS, AMERICA, AND THE WORLD

"A must-read for those determined to succeed!"

From a two-room school without running water, inside restrooms, electricity, or playground equipment to the chief social work position of the nation, the U.S. Department of State, the White House, and travels around the world, conferring with national leaders and serving mankind. What does it take? PERSEVERANCE!

Persevere!

CE Hodges 7/24/15

CLARENCE E. HODGES

CROSSBOOKS
PUBLISHING

CrossBooks™
A Division of LifeWay
1663 Liberty Drive
Bloomington, IN 47403
www.crossbooks.com
Phone: 1-866-879-0502

Scripture taken from the King James Version of the Bible.

First published by CrossBooks 03/14/2014

ISBN: 978-1-4627-3544-0 (sc)
ISBN: 978-1-4627-3543-3 (hc)
ISBN: 978-1-4627-3545-7 (e)

Printed in the United States of America.

This book is printed on acid-free paper.

CONTENTS

DEDICATION

This book is dedicated first to the memory and life-time service of Dr. Edward E. Cleveland who now sleeps in the hope of the soon-coming of his Lord. He served the world for sixty years as pastor, evangelist, administrator, author, and teacher of preachers. In his retirement years, we spent one day per week on a golf course where we talked, played and prayed and shared experiences of our services through various avenues to humankind in the name of our Lord and Savior. He urged me regularly to write this book sharing my up-stream experiences against the tide, persevering up the rough side of the mountain of life, achieving what few have achieved coming from where I started on the socio-economic, geo-political, ladder with its missing and broken rungs. I promised him that I would work on that project.

These former cotton-picking, bean-picking, tobacco-harvesting hands had not dreamed in those early years of writing at a computer about my standing before United States Senate committees being confirmed twice for presidential appointments to senior executive service which would take me around the world multiple times, sometimes in presidential aircraft, wrestling with diplomatic and domestic problems, sometimes at the White House, at the Capitol, and other executive agencies, managing billions of dollars and scores of thousands of workers in the interest of children, families, peace, human rights, economic development, and suffering citizens of the United States and the world. Most individuals have never met one person who has been confirmed for an executive position by the Senate one time. I certainly consider it a special honor to have been so confirmed without opposition two times.

Secondly, it is dedicated to Caleb Noah Hodges, my grandson, who continuously pursues academic eminence and athletic excellence, recognizing at the age of ten that if he perseveres, he can achieve greatness professionally and an Olympic gold medal in swimming. It is dedicated to Dr. Kiana Johnson, my granddaughter, who has already proven her excellence and perseverance serving as a social scientist at Purdue University and the University of Minnesota despite health and disability challenges which she has overcome since her early teen years. She has a diaphragm and breathing problem which, as far as medical science knows, affects only seventy-six other persons in the whole world. Other individuals deserve special honors, though not named, who are struggling or have struggled against poverty, neighborhood limitations, family constraints, illegal discrimination, and other restrictions beyond their control.

Lest the purpose is not clear throughout, it is not about one person, though Dr. Cleveland wanted it to be an autobiography. It tells how one person and others, have been extraordinarily blessed, in spite of obstacles and limitations, through relatives, educators, mentors, friends, educational and faith institutions, the grace of God, and perseverance. This book also contains information to and for the readers. Some specific identifying information has been altered to protect appropriate privacy. This project includes some of the good fortunes and benefits I have received from life and a sampling of some of the hardships and challenges. I have experienced but not mentioned the difficulties and trials of most and, therefore, can address them with empathy, compassion, and counsel.

My counsel to each is, you can if you think you can, do what never before has been done by man. As you think, you can. So persevere!

INTRODUCTION TO
THE BOOK AND THE AUTHOR

Clarence, I am glad you took the time to write this book. It is profitable reading for people in all stations of life. It certainly leads one to participate in some introspection and soul searching no matter the socioeconomic, intellectual and spiritual levels of the reader. The content of these pages certainly scream "it's what you do with what you have that makes you what you are." Hopefully some educators will discover it and couple it with their structured disciplines to teach leadership, humility, humaneness, charity, political savvy, faith, the importance and meaning of being a member of a family unit, and yes--PERSERVERANCE. (Mrs. Carolyn Stephens, retired educator and administrator, University City, Missouri)

PREFACE

Persevere begins with the scintillating aroma of Benjamin Franklin's *Autobiography*, a work written by a man who has acquired much wisdom in the process of industriously and unselfishly giving his service and talents to society; and having received more accolades than anyone of his lifetime, now looks back with gratification on a life well lived. But *Persevere* is much more than a journal of Clarence E. Hodges' colorful, estimable life; it is-- for want of a better word--a lesson-book, a guide book for living a rich, full life. Whether relating one of his many and varied experiences or sharing an anecdote from his own or another's experience, Hodges elucidates the lessons he has learned, sometimes homiletically, sometimes pragmatically, always with the goal of showing that life can be lived with purpose and success.

At the core of the work is the impressive record of public service to every sector of American society, including international relations. From his rookie days as a teenager in the military to his appointments in the White House and the General Conference of Seventh-day Adventists, supervisors and co-workers perceived his leadership skills and he was able to put them to use. Always a man of faith, prayer, and good humor, he soon learned that every challenge of his life's journey was a stepping stone or testing ground through which his loving heavenly Father prepared him for wider service and responsibility.

What Dr. Hodges humbly calls perseverance can also be called courage, resourcefulness, diligence, and faith. And to these he adds a refreshing attitude of gratitude, firm belief in providential direction at every stage of his life, and love for family and humanity.

As Hodges tells his amazing stories of a stellar upward climb from humble beginnings to national prominence, there is constant evidence of his enthusiasm for life and its possibilities, delight in happy results for integrity, perspicacity and hard work, joy in accomplishments, gratitude for support of family and others, and unfailing wonder at God's remarkable goodness. *Persevere* is heartwarming and inspirational, instructive and admonitory. The author's insight is matched with his shrewdness in appraising human nature and his kindness and compassion for even those who chose to perceive him as an enemy. Thank you for the inspiration, Dr. Hodges.

Lela M. Gooding, Ph.D.
Professor of English, Oakwood University
Huntsville, Alabama

Chapter One

MIRACLES START HERE

Miracles must start somewhere and for most of us it starts at conception. We may debate the issue of the chicken and the egg forever but humankind can rightfully claim little more credit than the chicken and the rooster. We cannot make it happen nor do we really understand what and why it happens or why most times, it does not happen. The point is, each one of us started with a miracle. After conception there is a gestation period of approximately nine months where there is not much direct motherly control over what happens in the growth and development of the sperm and ovum. Human decisions do not determine what happens and when it happens regarding that fortunate embryo and fetus in that uterus. For this little fellow, there was persistence on his part and his perseverance was rewarded with a compassionate slap on the bottom. This miracle bundle lodged an official complaint with all that his lungs could muster. Thus the celebration of the birth of Clarence Eugene Hodges had begun.

This miracle was special as there was so much information wrapped up in this little bundle which was different or arranged differently from any other person on Planet Earth. His DNA included 34 million digits of data in each chromosome, with 48 chromosomes per cell and with provisions for the development of 120 trillion cells. With all this and the eleven systems which already composed his little body, he was a certified miracle of miracles that humankind could not fully explain. But this little bundle of joy was not satisfied with being a typical miraculous birth, subject to live or die, based on his environment and his response to that environment.

Within a few months, his contaminated earthly environment had forced his little body to exhibit signs and symptoms which his country doctor did not understand and was challenged in identifying a diagnosis or a treatment plan. His hopeless words to the mother was, "If this child cries during the next two weeks, he will die." What sick child under a year old could go for two weeks without crying? The mother could not go for two weeks without crying over a child whose illness had stumped the only doctor in this small country town. But Grandmother Beatrice could pray; Mother Alphine could rock and sing to him, and three aunts, Trumiller Laura, and Arie, could walk and talk to him so that he could sense the power of love 24/7. And he could persevere and hold on hour by hour until someone shouted, "the two weeks are over and my baby has not cried." There were no doubts about a God in Heaven in that family and whenever there was a problem, especially with this miracle baby, all were reminded of the miracle of two weeks.

Well, another challenge did surface which led some to ask, "Did God bring him this far to leave him?" Grandmother Beatrice said, "I will answer that for all this family." Well, she was so thin that she was seldom called Bea for short. Her sisters, Nancy, Polly, and Effie called her "Gnat." However, when she spoke, she was never loud but everybody listened. The new challenge before the family and the physician developed while Mother was doing laundry outside. There was a time when that is where laundry was done whether the weather was hot or cold. Three year old Clarence had gone inside to get warm and got too close to the fireplace. He ran out the front door and by the time Mother could reach him and extinguish the burning clothes, the fire had cooked the muscle in his left leg. The doctor said he would never walk again. Grandmother said, "That is a decision for God to make." By the time he was six years old, not only was he walking, he was the fastest runner in the first grade. Miracle after miracle, after miracle, perseverance proved rewarding as perseverance represents faith and faith represents power and miracles.

It was interesting that no one thought too much of the little two-room Stoney Hill Elementary School Clarence attended. It had no electricity, no central heating system, no running water or indoor restrooms. This was a North Carolina school for "Colored children." They did not need much education because they would not achieve much. Their text books had other children's names in them because they had been used by the students at Belfast Elementary School two miles down the highway. The school buses were also hand-me-downs. The playground equipment, what little they had, was made by the children and their older brothers. When the Belfast buses passed, those students often would laugh and predict no achievement by the Stoney Hill students. The Belfast School also had a safety walk painted across the highway so when their balls were hit across the traffic, cars and trucks would stop and wait for those students to run and retrieve their balls in accordance with the highway signs. But Stoney Hill students had to be very careful if they crossed that highway even to board the school bus. There was no safety walk. Traffic did not slow down.

Perhaps some of those students from the Belfast School read the area newspaper, the Goldsboro News Argus, in May of 2003, when Dr. Clarence E. Hodges was featured on the front page of the Sunday paper with reports of his matriculating at prestigious educational institutions beyond their reach including a fellowship at Yale University and serving as a senior staff member in the United States Senate and as a senior executive at the United States Department of Health and Human Services, the State Department, and the White House. Just perhaps some may have read of his travels around the world as a senior diplomat, representing the Secretary of State, the American People, and the President of the United States. And some of the religious leaders of Wayne County may have read where he was ordained to the Gospel Ministry by the General Conference in Silver Spring, Maryland, and has preached the gospel to multiple denominations in Africa, Europe, Asia, South America, Canada, and the United States. This only goes to say that miracles never cease when we trust our awesome God and seek to serve Him by serving His children.

It is good to have diversions from work such as hobbies and activities for others with special needs. Gardening is a great stress reliever for some and jogging for some others. I have used multiple escapes from the ordinary. I bought a new house with an unfinished basement when I moved to Lincoln, Nebraska. I decided to finish the basement during my discretionary time. I had never done anything like this before so I got books from the library and talked with specialists at a home improvement store. It required careful reading and perseverance. I finished the project doing all the work except bathroom plumbing for commode and whirlpool tub. The drywall, ceiling, electrical circuits, wiring, and switches were challenging but rewarding when finished. Carpeting and painting were fairly simple. The inspectors had a reputation for being tough. I delayed informing that office of my status. My wife called one day to inform me that the inspector was there to see the work and to determine if it were in compliance with city codes. I could do nothing but give him access. He called me when he finished checking everything and advised that everything was in order except the bathroom exhaust fan was not working. I told him I had unplugged it. He plugged in the power cord and informed me that I had passed the inspection with a job well done. I wiped my brow and thanked him. This was a different kind of miracle but a miracle none the less.

I have experienced other housing miracles regarding buying and selling. A friend agreed to purchase my house with an occupancy date six months away. Five months passed and I still did not have a new house for my family. He was to move in on a Friday and I was searching the newspaper on that Thursday night. I located what we wanted and called the owner who was handling the sale. The electricity was off but we met with flashlights. We negotiated the sale, agreed for my occupancy the next day, met and signed all papers pending later closing, and we moved with the same truck my friend used for moving into the house I sold to him. Within twenty hours of the time I discovered the house for sale, I had moved in. I had some real estate sales experience and the seller had some knowledge so we could do what would not have been done by a broker. Later, I was selling a house in Maryland before moving to Nebraska. My wife suggested one of the largest broker chains in the country with whom I had a real estate license. I disagreed and called the small firm which sold me the house in the first place. The lady broker-owner came out and persuaded me to increase the asking price considerably which I did. As I took her around showing all the desirables, she shared that she wanted to buy that house when she sold it to me. I began to talk to her about the benefits and she agreed to make the purchase at the increased price and with no commission going to her. What a surprise deal of a deal. I did not have to put up a sign. Miracles happen in response to faith and perseverance.

Each experience needing a special solution or miracle, prepared the way for the next special need or miracle. As we pay more attention to unanticipated or unusual achievements, we should start anticipating the unusual and even the unbelievable from the scientific perspective. I owned a large luxury automobile like those used by government officials in Washington. I discovered an oil warning light problem which suggested the possibility of a serious problem. I checked with the service manager at my dealership and was told it could be a defective oil pump which would cost $30 as a part and a few hundred dollars for labor. I bought the part, picked up an auto repair manual from the library and proceeded to do the job. There was no need to rush as I had an extra automobile. I had to drain the oil, elevate the front end, detach and elevate the engine which had to be partially removed from the auto so the oil pan cover could be removed. After that, I could remove the oil pump, install the new pump, replace and seal the oil pan cover, lower the auto for resting on its wheels, lower the engine back in place, re-anchor all that had been disconnected, and refill the oil reservoir. I did not try starting it up right away as I was not ready for a big disappointment. My mechanical-minded son expressed his doubts that I could do it all. I tried to interest my sons in auto service and repair early as I learned at my military base hobby shop. I started it up later and it purred like a kitten with no leakage and no warning light. The feeling was great. Perseverance had spelled success again.

I was selling another house in Maryland preparatory to my retirement move to Alabama. I had contracted for building in Alabama and the date was getting close for completion. Legal issues had arisen in my Maryland subdivision where no house could be sold without the purchaser paying a large amount down, between 25% and 50% depending on some specifics regarding my lot and other specifics regarding the purchaser. There were zoning and property line issues that had to be corrected. No houses were being sold in the total community. I had would-be purchasers who could not meet those stiff down payment qualifications. My broker called one evening and stated he had a purchaser and we should quickly prepare for his occupancy. I questioned if he could qualify. I did not want to repeat the previous disappointments. He said, this sale is going through. The buyer does not have to qualify. He is paying cash. This was extraordinary that a purchaser wanted to pay cash and was ready to complete the deal.

This was very special that of all the houses available for sale, this buyer wanted my house. This also borders on miraculous. We closed the purchase in Alabama on Thursday and our furniture was delivered on Friday. I returned to Maryland on Monday and closed the sale there on Tuesday. Should I ever give up on miracles? I do not think so!

You can if you think you can; do what was never before done by man. As you think, you can. If you think you can, you will persevere and if you persevere, the chances are good that you will succeed.

Chapter Two

FAITH, FAMILY, AND FRIENDS

I have discovered that there is nothing more important in my life than faith. There are those who could probably identify many other resources which they would consider more important than faith. Some might place health above faith in importance. But for my life, when I have had health challenges and problems, faith was always a major contributor to my good health and healing. For others, education, employment, and financial resources are most important in their lives. Again, my life has been fraught with problems, issues, and needs in these areas and faith produced hope, assistance, assurance, strategies, and solutions.

Family is also very important even though some families have turned their backs to family members in need, or family members who have created problems for themselves, made unwise decisions, or for other reasons need "another" chance. In other words, some families have not exercised as much patience as some of the members needed. I am pleased to report that my family members have been available when needed. If they are not available when needed or if they are not patient and understanding, are they of value as relatives?

My family is partially responsible for my faith and our faith is largely responsible for the love which makes the family of great value to each member. Without faith, there would be no family as we know it. With faith, we can live happily together forever. And that is just what we plan to do.

I was very fortunate to have been born into a very loving family. Resources were limited but love was unlimited. My dad was sent to war before I was old enough to recognize and remember him. My earliest memory of him was when I was about five years of age. I had a photo of him in uniform which I valued until I left home for my military uniform. Most family photos also disappeared in moves and with different family members borrowing from the few available during the WWII and Korean war years. Dad never returned to the family after the war but did contribute some financial support. When I speak of a close loving family, I am referring to my mom, her three sisters and three brothers, her mother (my grandmother) and her three sisters and two brothers, and all the children born to the marriages of all those brothers and sisters. I had one brother, Leonard, two years older than I who was more mature than his age. He was truly a big brother, always helping his little brother. My mother's dad died when she was a child and her mom remarried so she had a step-father who was a caring grandfather. My dad's mom died shortly before my birth. My dad and his relatives lived in another city but they visited periodically and we at times visited them. But those who were closest emotionally were my mom's relatives who lived closest. Where resources were limited, transportation was limited and therefore, opportunities for traveling significant distances were limited.

One aunt, Arie Whitley, lived closest to us and had children my age and younger. We were, therefore, very close. She claimed part of the credit for me living through sickness as a baby. The doctor had me on a strict liquid diet and she secretly gave me light solid fruits and vegetables which she said contributed to my health and healing. My maternal grandmother, Beatrice, was thin but a giant of a woman. She had character, wisdom, and more than enough love to share with all her children and grandchildren. She was also very spiritual and a very compassionate person toward other relatives, friends and strangers. She had strong leadership skills and led the family in paths of integrity, responsibility, faith, and kindness. My grandfather, Clarence, died as grandmother Beatrice was giving birth to their only son, Clarence. She was not able to attend her husband's funeral so the undertaker drove the funeral car to the house before the funeral for her to get one last view of him. She was fortunate in that she did not have to worry about food or shelter for herself and her three children. My great grandfather, her dad, was owner of the plantation which had much land and several farm houses, one of which was occupied by my grandparents.

The great grandfather was the son of Lafayette Coley. It was assumed Lafayette would name his son, Lafayette, Jr. but, out of his love for freedom, he named his son Christopher Columbus who was viewed as a symbol of freedom. However, Christopher named his son Lafayette out of his love and admiration for his dad. Christopher was a very successful farmer with much farm land and fruit orchards. His main house or "big house" still stands and had a self-contained electric plant while other houses in the area had kerosene lamps etc. He was known by his initials, "Three Cs." Every Coley I have ever met acknowledged roots back to Wayne County, North Carolina, and to my great grandfather. There probably are some relatives who are older than I but I do not know them so I am the senior patriarch.

After the death of Clarence, my grandmother married Brodie who was a sharecropper. He chose not to live on my great grandfather's plantation. He had strength that complimented my grandmother's. But they both had clear understandings of male roles and female roles. This made a perfect match where there was no noticeable conflict. He did have conflicts with the owner of his farm. He threw a pitchfork barely missing the owner once with the pitchfork sticking into the side of a barn. On another occasion, he threw a hammer at the owner and the owner only came to my grandmother complaining that her husband had lost his mind. And did I mention that the owner was also a deputy sheriff with a small handgun on his side? He would participate in moonshine raids and share with my grandfather some of the best liquor that the sheriffs kept for themselves. I do not know why my grandfather attempted violent actions toward his landlord but apparently, the landlord was in the wrong since he never retaliated. Farm owners could get away with murder with a share-cropper acting so disrespectfully, not to mention a deputy sheriff. A gentleman living on the other side of the tracks, physically and figuratively, once claimed that I had put a dent in his car with my bicycle and took me to my grandfather's home for payment of the damage. He had his children with him to show them how to handle those of us on the poor side of the tracks. My grandfather was not a Christian and when I said I did not touch his car, the gentleman was cursed out and ordered out of my grandfather's driveway. The gentleman stated he would return with the sheriff and my grandfather said he did not fear the sheriff and that he would not allow the sheriff on his property. The gentleman never returned and nothing else was heard of the automobile dent. My grandfather's body lived on the "other side of the tracks" but his mind did not. I learned from my grandfather and others not to be intimidated by race or economics. It is good to know that you have family protection when a situation is beyond your capacity.

One of my aunts was married to a gentleman who sometimes drank too much moonshine. On one occasion he became violent and abusive to my aunt. My uncle, her brother, promptly went to their home where her husband, two brothers, and some of his friends were present. My uncle announced no one would get away with mistreating his sister as he grabbed his brother-in-law and proceeded to brutalize him. The brothers and friends made no moves to protect their brother as he apologized profusely. My uncle left him with broken ribs and black eyes. I do not promote violence but I do believe if more men made it clear that they would never tolerate violence against their sisters, daughters, and mothers, there would be less domestic violence in this country and the world. Love for those who cannot protect themselves will intercede for peace and that love should start in families.

Family members are a potential source of security and love to each other. And the time comes when that concept must be executed for other family members, including members of the broader family of mankind. It is great to see strangers stand up and stand in for strangers. It was hard to see my grandmother laid to rest in 1966 and my mom in 1997 where they lived far from me in North Carolina. But all that was made easier with my loving and caring cousins living nearby. And even their unrelated neighbors displayed love sometimes not seen in some families. My mother, her sister, and my grandmother lived within two blocks of each other and were known and loved throughout the neighborhood. They meant so much to so many, both within the family and beyond. They loved to serve and served with compassion. We need our aging relatives even when they need us and we are never prepared to let them go. We should be thankful for memories and take advantage of opportunities to build good memories before it is too late. The same is true of my only brother, Leonard. He was a giant of a man even when he was a teenager. He had knowledge, wisdom and compassion beyond his years. His wife, Elassie, and their children Lynda Renee and Eric Eugene, have great memories along with a wounded heart which can never fully heal in this life.

My wife, Yvonne, and I have four loving children. One of my daughters has expressed her appreciation for some of my friends who are seen as good people, considerate, compassionate individuals of integrity and substance. But on one occasion, she questioned why I maintained relationships with some persons who, on occasions, have displayed poor judgment or failed in some aspects of life. I shared with her my philosophy in that regard, that if I could not be a good friend when and if they needed a friend, they did not need me as a friend at all. One should seek to plan in such a manner, that they would never need to lean on a friend and should guard against over-dependency. However, as one popular song suggests, everybody may at some point, need someone to lean on.

I was driving my new automobile from St. Louis to Denver on a cold day in January. Before reaching Kansas City, it started to rain and the rain soon turned to snow and sleet. It was getting bad in Topeka and we were in a full blizzard near Salina, Kansas. I was taking some teenagers to participate in an oratorical contest. One was driving very well until we experienced some slipping and sliding. We decided that I should drive and that went well until we experienced a consistent bump from the rear. Yes, we had a flat tire probably from the salt and sand with some debris, being spread by highway trucks. I got out to change the tire but I was too cold by the time I unbolted the tire from its anchor. As I got back in the warm auto, another driver pulled to my rear bumper. I opened my door to step out and he said to me, "Sport, you are not dressed for this weather. I'll change the tire for you." I wanted to tell him my name was not Sport but if he would change my tire, he could call me Sport. He then asked that I follow him to the Colorado state line. I followed his old Oldsmobile until we were stopped as the highway was closed by state troopers at the state line. At that point, the old Oldsmobile disappeared. There was no road to the right or left. Some thought the stranger was an angel. We were extremely grateful as we were soon on our way. The highway workers had done their job. Whether an angel or a stranger, the driver of the old Oldsmobile represented a friendly response and a faith response.

I parked my auto on a wide, busy street in St. Louis one beautiful day, and as I started to walk across at the intersection, I heard the screeching tires of a speeding station wagon. I observed a bundle underneath, and noticed the children at play were screaming and running so I walked over. An eight year old lad had been hit and was underneath the station wagon. The police came and we got the child into an emergency vehicle. The boy's mother was summoned but the police determined she was of no value then due to substance abuse. They asked if I could ride in the emergency vehicle and help keep the child calm. I agreed and soon we were at Children's Hospital after a most reckless high speed ride on both sides of the street and on the side walk but this was justified by the seriousness of the child's injuries. At the hospital, the young fellow was identified as an out-patient who had a short life expectancy. I stayed with him for a while and returned frequently to visit him with gifts and hope from stories of miracles and faith. I also visited the mother and family and sought to encourage and counsel them. The day came when the traction and casts and previous fears of life expectancy were all past. He was released and playing at my home with my children. Months passed and they moved to another state. But before they moved, a seed of faith was planted and fruit was yielded. They now believe in miracles.

We may never know when we may need someone to lean on and family and friends may not be available or able. I was blessed in being able to come to the aid of this child and his family. Family relationships may be extended to the family of humankind in order to embrace strangers. Again, faith is never to be excluded even though you may not be able to depend on families of faith sometimes. However, there is always Someone we can count on if we have faith.

As Commissioner for the Administration for Children, Youth and Families, I had a responsibility for funding special programs at hospitals for children around the country. As I visited such, I encountered causes for happiness and for sadness. There are so many children with illnesses and disabilities who are happy and hopeful, never giving up on love and future opportunities to serve. There are also too many who are victims of child abuse and neglect who have been victims at the hands of those who should have been nurturing, protecting, and caring for them. Some have been tortured. Some have been denied food, clothing, and education. Society has to do more to protect and provide for all our children.

My daughter, Cassandra, screamed one night and came running to me in another section of the house. Someone was at her bedroom window. I ran outside with some visible protection to scare the prowler so he would never do that again. The next night, she came quietly to me and reported that he was back at the window again. She added that she had told her brother, Courtney, and that he had already gone out to apprehend this person. I then heard Courtney order the trespasser to lie down on the ground with threats of bodily harm. It turned out to be a young man of the neighborhood. I got his name and his parents' phone number and called his dad. My wife called the police. The father stated the young man would not listen to him so let the police handle it. This is another example of family love with my son intervening and an example of weak family ties with the young prowler. Some persons wonder how Cassandra and Courtney, now adults and living in distant cities, can visit their mother and me so often from considerable differences. Cassandra is a dentist in Chicago and I am one of her patients. She comes to see her parents and to take care of her father's dental issues. She also has a business where she has invented a tooth paste and dental rinse for healthy gums and teeth. These are excellent products for those who want healthy gums and teeth. Courtney has his own business, marketing, installing, servicing, and repairing dental equipment in Baltimore and surrounding towns in the Washington, DC area. He has flexibility which will allow him to check on his parents and use his many skills of maintaining and repairing. Isn't family a tremendous blessing? He also gladly assists, without charge, other seniors in need of his skills. Other family members of sisters-in-law, nieces, nephews, and cousins are as dear as they come and they acknowledge me as the old patriarch of the family. And my daughter (cousin), Alice Whitley Crawford and her sisters cared for my sick mother in North Carolina when I could not, with the love of a daughter. There are many friends who are closer than biological relatives in some families. I am referred to as uncle by children of this large network and I am honored by these loving relationships. They keep me informed on Facebook.

My older son, Clarence, has spent the last 15 years in South Korea teaching English, at the university level, to young Koreans and to businessmen who wish to expand their business relations into the United States. Clarence has developed many strong ties within the international family of humankind and he has found this to be very rewarding. He has established an English-speaking community of faith. This has been very challenging with him working long hours, helping children, youth, and families grow as a part of the global family of faith. My younger daughter, Cathleen, visits regularly also and stays longer because she comes less often. She is a lobbyist and real estate professional with some scheduling flexibility. Her husband, Jason DeLoach, comes as his schedule allows a busy recognized and honored "top 100 attorneys of the Washington, DC area."

If the family had not been created from the beginning, I would invent it from all its perspectives. This would make me the richest and happiest person on Planet Earth. Without the wealth, I can still be one of the happiest because of my family and the family of humankind. This is particularly true with most families when sickness and death come. My children and my wife's family gathered in St. Louis for the funeral of my mother-in-law. It was good to see those whom we had not seen for years. My son Clarence was there from Korea. My urologist had asked me to call him at that time for the results of my prostate biopsy. I called and he gave me the news that men over 50 fear they will someday hear. We now had another reason to press together as a family. My immediate family and some in-laws gathered around me as my sister-in-law, Eileen Nelson, prayed for my health and traveling mercies for us and others who were departing for home. We gave our good bye hugs to Clarence and others and started our trips.

Weeks of radiation therapy and radiation seeds progressed as I continued to work and kept speaking engagements and out-of-state appointments. Periodic exams indicated progress as desired and now 13 years later, the recent PSA reading was 0.00. Ample fruits, vegetables, water, exercise, fresh air, rest, prayer, temperance with that which is good and avoidance of that which is not will help with all our health challenges. Families can give that valuable loving support, encouraging each other in doing and living good, and minimizing stress.

President Obama shares an experience which illustrates a very special role for families. He, as U.S. Senator, had done some international travel with the chairman of the Senate Foreign Relations Committee, Senator Dick Lugar, and they were holding special hearings which covered some aspects of their travels to Russia. Senator Obama called his wife, Michelle, with some excitement within his always cool personality. He shared how impressed others were with the success he and Senator Lugar encountered. Issues of arms control and stockpiles of nuclear weapons were important to him and the nation but Michelle interrupted stating that there were ants in the house. Before he could resume, she told him to stop by a store and pick up some ant traps. She then told him that she had a doctor's appointment for the daughters. She then reminded him that she loved him but had to go. (Barack Obama, The Audacity of Hope, Crown Publishers, p. 326) Family members are better at keeping our feet on the ground and our heads out of the clouds than anyone else. How many successes have been turned into failures by not listening to our wives! I say wives because men are far more guilty of that weakness than are women. The Roman leader Pilate did not listen to his wife. Before the ladies take this too far, I must remind all that Adam did listen to Eve and so did Abraham regretfully listen to Sarah.

Chapter Three

LEADERSHIP

Military Service Opportunities

My first real leadership opportunities came when I enlisted in the United States Air Force as a teenager. I was sent to Lackland Air Force Base in San Antonio, Texas, for basic training. We were assigned in groups, squads, (12 per squad) with four squads in a barracks and several barracks within a squadron. I was the youngest in my 12 man squad and, in fact, the youngest in my whole squadron. For some reason, the senior instructor interviewed me to determine if I might have leadership qualities. When he discovered that I had learned military drilling (marching) while in high school, I was selected as one of the four squad leaders. Squad leaders were given a stripe from the beginning to indicate that leadership role. Squad leaders made sure their squads were ready for all scheduled activities from rising in the morning to lights out at night. We marched our squads to the dining hall for meals and back to the barracks after meals unless the instructors had other activities scheduled at those times. This provided an excellent opportunity for me to develop and display military leadership skills on a daily basis. My North Carolina background was not quite ready for leadership and giving orders without regard for race but I quickly caught on and enjoyed the position of barking out orders and helping other recruits to learn the basics of drilling and marching. Instructors did the real instructing while the squad leaders marched their squads to and from meals and a few other places. We could also assist those who needed extra instructions and practice on salutes and more complex maneuvers.

My size could never command attention at 5'8" and 150 pounds, but my voice could be deep and loud enough to make up for that. In addition, growing up with my older and larger brother, Leonard, gave me some preparatory advantages. He was always about the best at everything he did from academics and athletics to band instruments and speaking. I was a good student of his. I followed him in playing the large base horn in our high school band and that gave me an easy and preferred assignment in the basic training Air Force drum and bugle corps. In addition, he was a great wrestler. He mastered all the maneuvers and holds of professional wrestlers as seen on TV and he taught me how to take care of myself if challenged by larger individuals or even groups. I supplemented his instructions with studies in judo and jujitsu.

My senior instructor in Air Force basic training had been a professional wrestler and was about 6'4" and 265 pounds. With some of the larger trainees, he displayed some of his skills and some others joined in with others in a little wrestling fun after our assignments were done. I participated with some of the fellows my size but never got the attention of the former professional. After I bested and surprised a few one evening inside the barracks, they told the senior instructor that I was a former YMCA wrestling champ and claimed I could defeat anybody any size. That was not true. I had never entered a YMCA and made no claims about my ability. However, the instructor came after me and demanded that I show what I could do. I was that small teenager and knew I could not compete with that former pro so I ran from him in that open bay barracks behind bunk beds, between beds, and over beds until he tried to slam me against the wall with a set of bunk beds. I dived on the bottom bunk and rolled off to the floor before he could figure out where I was. I quickly picked him up and dropped his big heavy body on the floor. The noise could be heard on the first floor though we were on the second. He and I had pushed the beds all out of order and the place looked a mess. The noise brought trainees up from the first floor to see what could be wrong. I had embarrassed the big man and he was determined to make me pay for that. He twisted my body in a hold which I could not escape. Even if I could have, I knew it would not be good for me to make him look bad - - - again. I acknowledged him as the undefeated champ but this was enough for me to put fear in the hearts of others who might have wanted to challenge me. Thus, my military leadership skills were enhanced and my voice was respected. I was learning, as a youngster, how to survive in a man's world filled with sharks, snakes, wolves, and crooks. I continue to pursue health and fitness with the principles of NEWSTART (Nutrition, Exercise, Water, Sunshine, Temperance, Air, Rest, and Trust). Recently, I surprised some exercisers at the health and fitness center I frequent when I ran on a treadmill up to 10.5 miles per hour at my very senior citizen age. I also walk when I play golf several times per week.

After my basic training at Lackland Air Force Base and my professional skill training as an officer personnel specialist at Scott Air Force Base in Illinois, I was sent to Schilling Air Force Base near Salina, Kansas. What did I do to deserve that forsaken open space with very little to do when off duty? Well, it was not as bad as was seen through the eyes of young military personnel. I had nothing to do with my spare time so I used it to pursue college studies and to perfect my work as a personnelist. My personal records were soon filled with letters of commendation and praise for my professionalism, quality performance, creativity, knowledge of military laws and regulations, and attitude. I set records on efficiency tests and felt that I could move up the career ladder with speed. But that was in 1959 and 1960. There was no Dr. Martin Luther King, Jr. or civil rights movement as far as the military was concerned so I was rewarded with commendations not promotions. I was good enough to determine which captains, majors, and colonels needed which training to keep all our bomber and tanker planes of the Strategic Air Command ready for any needs during the cold war. And I could conduct briefings for General James Wilson who would keep General Curtis Lemay informed so that we were not bluffing when President Eisenhower would stand up to Kruschev and let him know the United States could make toast of the Soviets if they ever pushed their luck.

I was learning how the games were played and how to make the best of a bad situation. All was not bad in human and race relations, however. I went to church for worship in the small town of Salina and found worship services were not segregated as in most parts of the country. I was given opportunities to serve in a white church and to exercise leadership skills. And, after church, I was invited into homes for lunch and at times we would go into the public park and show the rest of the community that some Christians were above race and racism.

These experiences helped me to live and work with ease across racial lines as did my work in the Air Force with responsibilities that kept me communicating with senior officers and persons in leadership roles who were not threatened by my growth, successes, and achievements. I learned quickly that it pays to be helpful to others. If you wait to make friends when you need them, you will have none when you need some to help you succeed. Johnny Collins was a real airman friend and we spent time together discussing issues of interest from Bible subjects to achievement in an unfair world. He was a draftsman with all the skills I would ever need in making various types of charts. When I needed charts, I never had to get in line with others. I could give him my request an evening after work and he would deliver it to me the next evening. I had an automobile and he did not. We helped each other. General Wilson could not believe how I could get such charts done, displaying all classified statistics he needed to know. They made it clear where we stood with combat crew personnel who could fly those big planes, refuel in air on a moment's notice, and drop a series of bombs in enemy territory like dropping peanuts an elephant's snout. Writing is an essential skill for leaders and I soon learned to write to the satisfaction of the general and all the senior officers I assisted in helping secure the training they wanted, the best assignments available, and the career development which would assure them of their goals. I helped them and if I needed them, I could count on them, especially for letters of appreciation and commendation.

I served under the supervision of one older captain who had missed some of his promotions. This made him require of me nothing short of perfection in my writing, my understanding and interpreting of laws and regulations. My interviewing and counseling skills were developed and my decision making on personnel requests and issues were trusted.

Serving God and Country

However, on the church issue, I soon discovered it was worth my time, energy, and expense to travel weekly eighty-five miles to Wichita, Kansas, to a church of my worship style. This was delightful. I was young and single and there were attractive young ladies which were glad to make my acquaintance. Pastor and Mrs. Joseph LeCount Butler were most helpful and made sure appropriate families were most hospitable for lunches and even overnight stays. If all churches showed such love and compassion, youth would remain more faithful and guests would respond more favorably. This spirit of fellowship and friendship continued after I was married and brought my wife, Yvonne, to Kansas from St. Louis. For two years, until I completed my military service, we would drive to Wichita and spend all day for church, religious, and social activities and never once did we have to purchase a meal or go to a hotel if we decided to spend a night.

When I left the military and we relocated to St. Louis, Missouri, my wife's hometown. The pastor there, D.B. Reid, was just as helpful and even more determined to have me to organize and provide leadership for special youth initiatives and programs. He assisted in my growth and development in every area. He trusted me from age 20 and I worked hard to never disappoint him. My leadership with youth, young adults, and senior citizens was blessed with strong support from every age group. Youth group federations and congresses were organized to serve youth from several communities and cities of multiple states. W.W. Fordham, the Central States Conference president, was just as supportive and helped me to develop political skills for use in the church and in the community on a multi-state basis. I was involved in community service, youth development, and educational activities affecting the states of Missouri, Kansas, Nebraska, Colorado, and Iowa. I used my summer vacations to serve as boys director at Camp Shady Hill summer camp near Kansas City, Kansas. Here I learned that work can be fun even if it is as a volunteer. It is amazing how much one can learn in volunteer assignments which can contribute to resumes and success in other professional and paraprofessional positions. Educational, recreational, and inspirational activities with youth can keep adults physically, mentally, and morally fit. My own children were involved at an early age and developed with older youth to be an asset to larger communities.

I learned from many enjoyable and challenging experiences which have benefitted me to this day. My local experience as a Master Guide and Pathfinder leader (similar to scouting programs) helped me to serve effectively in camping programs. And my military experience allowed me to introduce military discipline and marching. But one young person at camp, Fred, was the only one from his hometown. During his first year he was a stranger. I assigned others to help him adjust and fit in but he was a complainer and not cooperative. One day, I encountered him alone and decided to talk with him casually to encourage him to get more out of camping. He started complaining about everything and everybody. I lifted him by his jacket, held him against a wall, told him I had heard enough of his negativity, that he had to put up with everything everybody else had to endure and he was getting no more breaks from me. I dropped him to the ground and ordered him to get with his group. He ran as he answered, yes sir. He started following me whenever he could. There were no more complaints and he volunteered for extra work assigned to his group. He was later voted the number one male camper by all the boys. He responded to a little tough love and some special attention. He also got praise when he did well. I discovered adults are the same as children. They need to know the boundaries and the consequences of positive and negative behavior. The sooner they learn, the better they respond.

I took my military writing experience into other communities in which I lived and served. This includes the development and publishing many newsletters for both civic and professional communications. I also served as a regular columnist for Message Magazine, Review and Herald Leadership, St. Louis Argus, St. Louis American, and Indianapolis Recorder. I have authored numerous articles (Extended Remarks) for the U.S. Congressional Record.

My service with youth involved several different settings. Bobby was an excellent teenager. I enjoyed working with his brothers and sisters in a large group. I looked to him as a good influence on others. I taught him along with others to drive and I could always trust him to respond quickly to directives. After I had moved away and had not seen him for years, I ran into him in the St. Louis airport where he was an agent for TWA. We had a delightful visit but he complained that I should have been flying first class. He then upgraded me to that level. Whenever I could fly through St. Louis, I arranged for a stop there. I always got my upgrades. On one occasion on my way to the West Coast, I was advised by two agents working together that Bobby was not working that day. I displayed my disappointment and they asked if they could help. I told them of my mentor relationship with Bobby when he was young and what a nice, responsible youth he was. I told them I needed an upgrade from Bobby. They were delighted to hear my praise of Bobby. They agreed with my compliments and said they would gladly give me that upgrade on behalf of Bobby. After many years, he got in touch with me recently and we talked on the phone for an hour, which is very long for me, expressing delight for those earlier years we spent together. He has excelled and he had me talk with his lovely wife who is also a tremendous person and nurse practitioner.

Another teenager, Jean, was a real jewel, with many talents. We both had interests in political issues and she enjoyed challenging my thoughts. After many years, we lived in the same city again. She became my wife's physician and my wife praises her to the stars for her professionalism and bedside manners. She and her husband are also known as outstanding Oakwood Church youth leaders with Pathfinders. Some months ago, I loaned her some resource materials which are difficult to acquire. They moved to another state but returned the materials with a note which read, in part, "Greetings to you and your wife. Thank you for sharing these resources with me. A special thank you for the mentoring over the years. You have been a blessing to so many, especially me. Love, Jean."

I mention these experiences, as the tip of the iceberg, to encourage other youth and adults to give some service to the youth of this nation and the world. You will never regret it and will be rewarded beyond financial compensation. The network just from those few years of service, reaches around the world as many of those youth are now making this a better world for the citizens of the world. I am indebted to professional youth leaders such as Joseph LeCount Butler, Dick Barron, and Sherman Cox for allowing me to serve and learn as boys' director when they were camp directors for many years, in the order listed, at Camp Shady Hill.

Adults can learn from children and the more educated can learn from the less educated. A genius can learn from a fool though the fool may learn nothing from the genius. And one will find more wisdom in the Bible than he may find in a scientific library. The book of Proverbs alone could have saved many highly educated professionals and world leaders from embarrassing indulgencies and failures. That's why the former Chief of Chaplains for the United States Navy who is currently Chaplain for the

United States Senate, Dr. Barry Black, states that he reads some portion of the book of Proverbs every day. Persevere!

Opportunities to Serve Humankind

My work in St. Louis moved from sales to social work. I had learned to interview and test well so when I encountered tests which were designed to keep the unprepared out of supervisory positions, I did very well and some very capable competition was screened out of my path. Some appeared more deserving than I even in my estimation. I moved upward as fast as the time requirements would allow so that each year, I was being promoted to higher positions with higher pay. I was told on several occasions that no one had moved upward as fast as I. I knew, though I had worked to prepare for moves, the moves were not based on my superior abilities. Others were talented and worthy also. Our efforts, faith, dependability, integrity, hard work, smart work, perseverance, positive attitudes, mentors, and friends gained by being supportive and helpful of others will make a difference. Friends and supporters included Congressman Bill Clay, Police Commissioner Clifton Gates, Mayor Al Cervantes, and political and civil rights activist Norman R. Seay. Norman was helpful and supportive in civil rights activities and employment. He was most influential in inner-city economic development and anti-poverty programs. Another key difference was that Heaven was blessing desirable traits, community support and the strong support of the religious community. Other decision makers also look for these traits. My blessings were therefore multiplied on a daily, monthly, and annual basis. My elevation was in the interest of serving others not for me to be the victor in some competitive events. Success is to be about service to others, especially the less fortunate. Anyone can persevere and follow these approaches and see the same results.

Positions, Promotions, and Doors of Opportunity

I moved from social case worker in the Missouri State Welfare system to senior social worker in 20 days with a retroactive promotion while still in orientation and technical training, and then to social work supervisor in one year (the youngest in the whole state). I passed the required exam and was on track for promotion to an administrative position over social work supervisors. I could not refuse a surprise offer to become director of social services for the Kinloch School District. Working with students, faculty, and families was a delight but another surprise offer as management analyst in the St. Louis/Federal Economic Opportunity Programs (Human Development Corporation) had unlimited opportunities for future national service. Within that system, I moved rapidly through a series promotions as Neighborhood Youth Corps director, New Careers Director, Deputy Director for Concentrated Employment Programs, and then to Executive Director for U.S. Department of Labor St. Louis Concentrated Employment Programs. This totaled nine upward positions within a period of approximately eight years. More opportunities were available, including the corporate sector as major corporations were being pressured to employ more minority executives. The sky is the limit. Persevere!

National Urban Fellowship

At that point, I did what few could understand as I left St. Louis to accept a National Urban Fellowship at Yale University in New Haven, Connecticut, in cooperation with Occidental College in Eagle Rock, California, and with collateral developmental and leadership responsibilities as a senior assistant to Indianapolis Mayor Richard G. Lugar. This fellowship was sponsored and supported by the U.S. Conference of Mayors and National League of Cities. This represents a ton of opportunities for networking and job opportunities upon completion. Within six months, my Indianapolis responsibilities were expanded with a major shift of authority and responsibility. With my commuting and academic pursuits at Occidental and Yale, and my substantial and ceremonial roles as Assistant to the Mayor, one would think my plate was full. However, after a few important successes for the mayor, he decided to hire me on the city's payroll as director for the city department of human resources as I continued my National Urban Fellowship responsibilities and studies. My position as Human Resources Director included responsibilities for social services, employment and training, community health centers, neighborhood development, and community relations. Learning national programs, laws and regulations, local politics, essential relationships, complex systems was demanding. Making changes to benefit people and neighborhoods that had been ignored and underserved for decades and lifetimes were exciting. That was much for one person and I also served in the local church. I did it all with continuous praise from the mayor and community leaders, by the grace of God. I received my masters degree and continued my pursuit for a Ph.D. in politics and public administration. I shall appreciate the National Urban Fellows program forever for its benefits to all they have served and for the benefits to the nation.

"National Urban Fellows is one of the country's oldest and most prominent leadership development organizations for mid career public service professionals. Our mission is to develop accomplished and courageous professionals of all ethnic and racial backgrounds, particularly people of color and women, to be leaders and change agents in the public and nonprofit sectors, with a strong commitment to social justice and equity." (Miguel A. Garacia, Jr., President and CEO, National Urban Fellows)

I can look back and see some distant similarities between my movements and those of one of my highly admired government officials, General Colin Powell. In the early seventies, he was two years older than I and we both won very special fellowships. He was a White House Fellow, studying at George Washington University with links to the White House though he states he did not spend time there (photo page 19, My American Journey, Colon Powell). It is one of the most prestigious fellowships or scholarships one can secure. Some of the fellowships and scholars programs and institutes are more popular than others. But aspiring youth and mid-level managers who have an opportunity to compete for such should go for it, regardless of the institutions involved or making the offers. If one is interested in an academic and career fast-track, these fellowship and scholars programs present opportunities for graduate, doctoral, and post-doctoral academic achievement with tremendous career opportunities and networks beyond. General Powell had begun to soar in the military as a young Lieutenant Colonel earning $16,000 per year with a wife and family of three children (Ibid, p. 153). It is difficult to soar nationally in Indianapolis but the mayor bumped my salary to $21,000 which was good for the early and mid-seventies for my wife and family of four children. The upward bumping continued from Indianapolis to Washington.

Later, the General and I did some work at the White House and the Department of State. It was my privilege when I was at the State Department to invite General Powell to speak, at my National Leadership Conferences, to leaders from around the country on issues of national defense and international security. He was National Security Advisor to the President and was making an impact on global policies. The State Department, the Secretary of State, and I were honored by his participation and cooperation on diplomatic initiatives. Some of the other speakers I used annually and other special events at State Department forums included Secretary of State George P. Shultz, Secretary of State James A. Baker III, Middle East Ambassador Dennis Ross, members of Congress, and other leaders of the nation and the world. General Powell later became Secretary of State and probably could have become President had he chosen to do so. I mention this only to show how small the world is and how great the opportunities are if we serve and persevere in our service. Fellowships and scholars programs pay well while providing academic and professional experiences and they open doors with special opportunities. Internships are somewhat similar, usually for college students or those without professional experience. (See www.findinternships.com) They are good for college students but fellowships are for higher level achievers. The rules below are good for the attitudes of young and old.

Colin Powell's Rules:

1. It ain't as bad as you think. It will look better in the morning.
2. Get mad, then get over it.
3. Avoid having your ego so close to your position that when your position falls, your ego goes with it.
4. It can be done.
5. Be careful what you choose. You may get it.
6. Don't let adverse facts stand in the way of a good decision.
7. You can't make someone else's choices. You shouldn't let someone else make yours.

8. Check small things.
9. Share Credit.
10. Remain calm.
11. Have a vision. Be demanding.
12. Don't take counsel of your fears or naysayers.
13. Perpetual optimism is a force multiplier.

(My American Journey, Colin Powell, Random House, 1995, p. 613)

Fellowships provide educational opportunities, high level experience opportunities, and unlimited networking, however, career options are the goal and these options bring perks and unique benefits which should never be ignored. My sitting behind the big desk in the Oval Office talking with the real occupant of that chair and desk while he stood to the side; my flying in one of those presidential aircraft from country to country; going to bed as we fly; and even traveling here and there with a diplomatic passport from the United States of America; avoiding lines and security searches are honors that no one can claim they deserve. Many others who missed some special breaks have been just as deserving if not more so. The special honors are humbling and should lead the recipients to love to serve and to serve with love, and help others replace them, at the appropriate time, with excellence. And as we prepare to rise to high heights, let us prepare to return to common ground with attitudes of gratitude.

We need the best of leaders in our government at local, state, and national levels, however, the quality of elected officials seems to be diminishing. Too many choose not to go through the dirty political processes. Even the non-elected political processes are becoming too dirty and personal for too many would-be outstanding public servants. We can learn much from some outstanding non-elected government servants, such as Colin Powell. Richard Clarke has done well and he gives an example of another who has excelled.

"As a public servant, few have ever equaled Hyman Rickover, who served his nation for sixty-three years under thirteen Presidents, from Woodrow Wilson to Ronald Reagan. At the dawn of the nuclear age in the 1940s, Rickover understood better than anyone else the promise of a nuclear Navy. . . He demanded excellence from everyone around him, handpicking every single officer, and would go to somewhat unusual lengths to test them. . . . . He told one candidate to go stand in the closet and close the door and not to come out until Rickover came to get him. Rickover then left for the day. The next morning he walked into his office, opened the closet door and hired the young officer who had not budged all night. In the submarine community, it is widely reported that the young officer was Jimmy Carter. . . Today, Rickover's influence continues to be felt. . . Rickover outlined his management philosophy in a speech titled 'Doing a Job.' I tried to keep his points in mind as I attempted to manage programs from the White House. They could well be applied to most national security senior management positions today:

"People, not organizations or management systems, get things done.

"Management is hard work.

"Subordinates must be given authority and responsibility early in their careers.

"Get rid of formal job descriptions and organizational charts. Define responsibilities, but define them in a general way so that people are not circumscribed.

"Complex jobs cannot be accomplished effectively with transients. Short rotations ensure inexperience and nonaccountability.

"Don't downplay problems to try to save face.

"Flatten management structures, but empower the remaining managers and hold them responsible.

"Good ideas are not adopted automatically. They must be driven into practice with courageous impatience.

"The man in charge must concern himself with details. If he does not consider them important, neither will his subordinates.

"Develop simple and direct means for finding out what subordinates are doing and what the status of projects is.

"Don't let your inbox set your priorities. Unimportant but interesting trivia pass through every office.

"Check all work through independent and impartial review. In engineering and manufacturing, industry spends large slums on quality control but the concept of impartial reviews and oversight is important in other areas also.

"Important issues should be presented in writing. Nothing sharpens the thought process like writing down one's arguments."

(By Richard A. Clark, Your Government Failed You, Harper Collins Publishers, New York, 2008; 30 years of service at the White House, Pentagon, State Department, and intelligence community)

I personally recommend consideration of Admiral Rickover's management philosophy as stated above. Nonprofit, educational, social service, and volunteer organizations can also benefit from such. However, I would not choose to work for one who utilized a very odd selection tests such as that reportedly used for hiring Jimmy Carter. Nor would I choose to serve with one who micromanaged or demanded "loyalty of thought." This is particularly true where backgrounds, culture, and economic status differ.

Civil Rights Service

I was a victim of civil rights violations for all my childhood years, for all my adult years, plus all my total years. As a child, I was a victim of segregated public education up to and past the 1954 Topeka vs. Board of Education Supreme Court decision. Everything that was old, used, and could be passed down from white schools to black schools were passed down and often in poor condition. I drank from segregated public water fountains until I reached sixteen years of age. At that time, I launched my own protest initiative by drinking from the white fountains without swallowing all the water that reached my mouth. I had to take food out of fast food places while others could eat inside. I had to sit in the back of buses after purchasing tickets in "colored" waiting rooms.

Not only was the above true as a child but also when I was in the military and in uniform letting the world know that I was ready to sacrifice my life for my great country. On one occasion, while riding with four white military friends, I was denied service in a restaurant in President Truman's home town, Independence, Missouri, and had to wait outside in the hot automobile while the others enjoyed their meals inside the cool air conditioned diner.

I left the military 1960 and later joined the NAACP, the Congress of Racial Equality (CORE), Urban League, and the Black United Leadership Coalition. I was President of St. Louis CORE, vice president of St. Louis County NAACP, and Executive Director of the United Coalition. I worked well with all groups though some were considered "non-violent" and others "by-any-means-necessary." I did not preach non-violence and supported individuals responding to violence according to the dictates of their individual consciences. I was active in the Urban League with its interest in education, jobs, and business development. I deeply appreciate and support the Southern Poverty Law Center with its legal pursuit of justice in the criminal justice system. I was inspired daily by listening while driving to Martin Luther King, Jr. speeches on my 8-track sound system. I was accessible to the media and had opinions on all issues and, as such, benefitted from a lot of publicity, some negative and most positive. I authored weekly columns in Black newspapers, making sure my positions were reported in my own words. That's how I could be honest to my convictions regardless of whose administration employed me. It was clear that my religion, family, and race never took a back seat to a political agenda. That is true with ACLU also. I agree in general but not in conflict with religious liberty principles.

On one occasion, when I had demanded and received equal time following the major CBS radio talk show featuring the KKK representative for an hour, a caller threatened to chase me out of town. I assured the audience that if there was a chase involving him and me, he would be out front as the chasee and I would be the chaser. I had been through enough not to be intimidated and was prepared to protect my family and withstand the threats of hate-mongers. Those organizations that try to use fear and terror to achieve their goals are themselves fearful that those they hate will get ahead of them. They have little confidence in their talents, intellect, and ability to utilize reason so they turn to approaches grounded in ignorance and low self esteem. We need to help them overcome these self destructive approaches especially within the political and religious arenas. They hold our country down and discredit their God.

There were ugly times of threats in my civil rights activities but my only concern was for the safety of my wife and four young children. My wife called me at work one day informing me that she had received a call stating that my five year old daughter had been kidnapped from kindergarten. The police were notified but the school advised that my daughter was safe at school. I started providing my own armed protection for my daughter as she continued to walk to school alone. When I could not do that, my wife would transport her to and from school.

On one Saturday afternoon, the Chief of Detectives for St. Louis County, a very colorful hotshot cop, always in the news as a hero, knocked at my door with four other detectives. We visited briefly and he requested my permission for four detectives to spend the night in my living room with their car in my garage and my car on the street. Permission was granted but I was given only a partial, half believable reason. About midnight, my wife asked why the sound of metal banging against metal was coming from the living room. When I told her they were loading their high powered assault weapons, she became fearful and wondered if we should leave home. About 5:00 am, we heard their automobile speed out of our garage and driveway but never got any other reports. Was there danger, or was my house being bugged, or was there something else? We will never know.

It was my privilege to follow in the CORE leadership shoes of Congressman Bill Clay, other activists, and local political leaders including Norman R. Seay, Solomon Rooks, and Representative Ray Howard. I had proven my leadership as employment chairman negotiating and pressuring job agreements in the business community. Donald Gammon and I worked closely together when he was my vice president and he followed my presidency when I resigned and moved to Indianapolis. He and I are still friends and reflect at times on the good old days. I also served with Norman R. Seay to get Dr. King's birthday a holiday in St. Louis and to get a street named for his honor. A park has been named in Norman's honor. He and I also worked together in providing employment and training opportunities for the unemployed. He was my senior initially until he moved on to a career in creating and providing educational services. Later, when strong support developed across the country to make King's date of birth a holiday and a national commission was created by the president, I was appointed as cochairman of the International Affairs Committee with Ambassador Andrew Young at the request of Mrs. Coretta Scott King. When Ambassador Young could no longer serve, I was appointed chairman and travelled to various countries of the world promoting Dr. King's birthday as a national holiday. Many country leaders responded with a variety of memorial activities in honor of Dr. King. While I served in a leadership capacity at the U.S. Department of State, the Secretary of State, George Shultz, and I co-hosted an international reception honoring the memory of Dr. King and the King family, involving ambassadors from countries of Africa, Europe, Australia, Asia, North America, South America, and the islands of the seas. Pastor Wintley Phipps made this event remind us of civil rights events of the past with a thought-provoking message and music from Heaven. The co-hosts and others also spoke.

At the time of my move from St. Louis, I was working on a St. Louis police department corruption case where one detective had made several arrests outside his district securing convictions for crimes which may have been committed by others. In one case, a person who had a connection to a murder was set free when the person with no connection and an alibi, was convicted. On another, a teenage member of my church was shot eighteen times. The shooter reportedly started shooting from inside his house through his screen door and walked outside and continued to shoot as the unarmed youth walked or ran down the sidewalk. The dead youth was accused of trying to break and enter while the owner sat looking out his front door with his rifle. The only weapon or burglary tool, allegedly, in the youth's possession was a screwdriver. The investigating detective was nearby but out of his district and built the case for justifiable homicide. A Catholic nun was working with me and she was reassigned to another parish in another state.

I moved from St. Louis to Indianapolis to accept the National Urban Fellows assignment, referred to above, living and working part time for the mayor in Indianapolis and living and studying part time in Connecticut and California. Some thought I was paid off to leave St. Louis and that corrupt policeman situation. However, I was under consideration for the outstanding fellowship with the mayor of Indianapolis and with collateral educational opportunities for several months before. That move involved a lengthy screening and selection process. Those who knew me and the mayor of Indianapolis knew we would never participate in any shady deal. We both had too much to gain and too much to lose for questionable acts.

My first challenge in the City of Indianapolis, as an urban fellow, was to solve a problem which appeared to be one of race in city government. The Sanitation Workers Union and minority workers in all divisions of the Department of Public Works were threatening to shut the city down with a strike the way similar employees had done in New York when John V. Lindsay was mayor of that great city, thus ending Mayor Lindsay's bright political career. Mountains of garbage were stacked on sidewalks with stench and rats in abundance. There was a similar problem which was being addressed by Dr. Martin Luther King, Jr. when he was assassinated in Memphis, Tennessee. Sanitation workers for many years had been victimized in all large cities and towns which looked to minorities to fill these less desirable positions. The mayor of Indianapolis had received a letter threatening to shut the city down until their complaints were resolved. The complaints were not specified. The mayor assigned me the task of determining the specific complaints and what he could do to satisfy those essential workers. The mayor was planning to run for the United States Senate and did not need labor strife and a shut-down of the city. I was given directions to the workers' meeting place and the key names with whom I needed to talk. I arrived at the meeting as a newcomer in town who knew no one.

As I arrived at the meeting place, the manager of the solid waste division was leaving. He had just told the workers that I had arrived but could do nothing as I knew nobody and nothing about the city and their issues. They, therefore, had no interest in wasting their time talking with me just to give the mayor more time to ignore them. I got their attention and assured them that I did not play games with serious issues and would not be used by the mayor if that was his intention. I promised them if they gave me legitimate problems, I would work with the mayor to make immediate changes or, if he was not serious, I would abandon the project. They opened up with a long list of serious grievances which they alleged had been ignored by the system designed to resolve such. The first problem, they stated, was the manager who told them to ignore me. They wanted minority supervision that understood their issues and would improve their working conditions. To make a long story short, I reported their concerns back to the mayor and told him how that supervisor had sought to undercut my efforts and the mayor's leadership. My advice was that he remove that supervisor and replace him with an African American who had years of experience and enjoyed the confidence of the employees. I submitted a quality name, Carlos, that would be acceptable to the employees. He was known and had some supervisory experience. The mayor directed me to prepare the correspondence for his signature to effect those changes for 8:00 am the next day. This was done. I now had the confidence of the workers, the attention of all six division managers, and the whole public works department. Within three days, three persons had been fired, others reassigned, and minority employees were being elevated. The manager of the liquid waste plant had served through three mayors and thought he was too powerful for the mayor to remove as he was managing a $300,000,000 upgrade of the liquid waste plant with a grant from the federal Environmental Protection Agency. He was removed, replaced, and made a consultant. EPA was not pleased but the U.S. President had already proclaimed Mayor Lugar as the outstanding mayor of the country. I met with all the leadership of the department. The director and the other managers apologized for some past behavior, stating they had families to feed and that they would gladly work with me to improve the department. The deputy mayor, Mike DeFabis, was very colorful and often used language stronger than that used by the mayor and me. He met one of those fired in the street who threatened to sue all of us to get his job back. The deputy mayor proceeded to curse him out in public, telling him to go ahead and sue and he would learn the lesson of his life. Some thought the deputy mayor was just more verbal with bluff. His being verbal did not hurt and there was no suit. The opposition got the message from several perspectives. Crime and mistreatment of others do not pay.

There was no strike and the union leadership requested a meeting with the mayor, deputy mayor and me. They arrived and presented awards to the three of us. That is when the mayor decided to appoint me as Director for the Department of Human Resources while keeping my position as Special Assistant to the Mayor. Our relationship was cemented forever. It was obvious that Heaven was on my side. I had not earned all the credit extended to me but I was enjoying it.

In Indianapolis, I was involved in every community and civil rights organization. I was very active in the NAACP. The president was my dentist. I kept him informed and he kept my teeth healthy and protected my name from any who might try to detract from my community commitment. I chaired the education committee for the Urban League seeking to protect the rights of young African American males in public schools. I was active in the Black Political Caucus which included most black elected officials, political and community activists, and government employees. Almost all of these identified themselves with the Democratic Party. To the amazement of most observers and the media, I was elected chairman of that group though I was a very public official in the Republican administration with Mayor Richard Lugar. I was seen as on the right side of all issues important to the inner-city community, regardless of where other political leaders stood. I put the community ahead of politics. My writing of a weekly column in a community newspaper was consistent with that stated commitment. Unlike most political employers, this mayor respected my right to voice a position that was not identical to his. We believed that if two persons agreed on everything, only one was thinking and only one mind was needed. If both did not have the same background and experiences, they could not think alike on everything.

After a few years, there was a hot political contest for a United States Senate seat. Mayor Lugar was challenging Senator Vance Hartke. A debate was requested to cover only employment issues and the proposed Full Employment Bill pending in Congress. It was to take place in Foster's Hotel and Lounge, a favorite meeting place in the inner city. The senator said he could not participate due to pressing business in Washington but he would send a representative who could fully represent him. The mayor stated he had a scheduling conflict but he would send a representative who could fully represent him. The decisions were made and approved. A brilliant, popular attorney who had been the state's nominee for attorney general for his political party was to represent Senator Hartke and I was to represent Mayor Lugar. A young female reporter for the popular WTLC Radio station was the moderator. The air was filled with excitement as my opponent was a skilled debater and I was known as public speaker and sometimes preacher at local churches.

What was not understood by Senator Hartke and his representative was that I had directed all the various employment and training programs sponsored by the U.S. Department of Labor in St. Louis for five years before moving to Indianapolis. I had written the proposals and the contracts. And as Director for the Indianapolis Department of Human Resources, I was responsible for the employment and training programs in Indianapolis. In all humility, I must acknowledge that I was the expert on employment and training programs. My opponent was, therefore, at a tremendous disadvantage since he had no in-depth knowledge of any employment and training programs at the federal funding and contracting level, the state employment offices, Urban League programs, programs for youth, skill training programs, retraining programs, ex-offender programs, long term unemployed issues, Economic Opportunity Programs, veterans assistance programs, opportunities for older Americans, or opportunities for welfare-public assistance recipients. I knew him to be an honorable and competent person and certainly did not wish to embarrass him. He was being misused by those who put him in that position and he was over-confident. However, it was my responsibility to educate all persons on all these issues without, in any way, exalting myself or displaying a condescending attitude.

Upon conclusion, I was congratulated by all, including my opponent, for having informed the public of the facts, issues, and viable solutions for employment and poverty problems. The radio station management called the moderator and advised her that the recorded debate would not be played later as previously announced, due to the lop-sided performance. This was in no way arranged by me and I did not deserve all the praise I received. It did show again that the powers of Heaven are involved in our successes and accomplishments and that we should be careful how we claim credit for that which we could never achieve on our own. Except for the grace of God, any of us can end up in an embarrassing position at any time.

My community activism impressed some very prominent Baptist ministers in Indianapolis. These included Reverend Mozel Sanders and Reverend Andrew Brown. These were super leaders and good friends of mine. Reverend Sanders provided the leadership for Opportunities Industrialization Centers (OIC) under the national leadership of Reverend Dr. Leon Sullivan; and Reverend Brown provided leadership for the Southern Christian Leadership Conference, first under Dr. King and then under Reverend Ralph D. Abernathy followed by Reverend Joseph Lowery. It was an honor for me to support their initiatives. Reverend Brown urged me to consider becoming the national director of Operation Breadbasket after Reverend Jesse Jackson resigned and started Operation PUSH. I assured him that I was interested. He arranged for me to meet with Reverend Joseph Lowery in Atlanta. I had an excellent meeting with Reverend Lowery (then president of SCLC) and the Reverend assured me that he wanted me to take the leadership of Operation Breadbasket. First, they needed to do some restructuring. However, they did not complete the restructuring and did not place it in the prominent role they desired before I was selected by the President of the United States for a national leadership position. I am sure my life would have been on a different track had we gone in that direction. I would have enjoyed it and would have worked hard to improve the quality of life of millions of disadvantaged families as I did in my federal government position. However, I have no regrets. I was honored to have been considered. It is good for young persons with ambition to keep options open and network with others who are making a difference for society.

Dr. Leon Sullivan was very active internationally in human rights issues and as a member of the General Motors Board of Directors. He worked to bring an end to apartheid in South Africa, primarily with his Sullivan Principles. He organized the first African, African American, others of African descent, and friends of Africa Summit in Abidjan, Cote d'Ivoire (Ivory Coast), West Africa, in 1991 in the interest of economic and social advancement. I was pleased to be a supporter and honored to be a speaker at this historic event. This and other initiatives have continued as a part of the Leon Sullivan Foundation since his passing in 2001.

For those with public service ambitions, I advise that they accept opportunities to develop public speaking skills. And don't expect or request fees for such during your learning phases. Churches, political groups, and civic organizations provide ample opportunities for development in this area. However, one should be careful to keep such communications short and informative. I would also suggest the avoidance of negativity. Politicians are usually too negative, too long, and too unbelievable. That is one reason I have little interest in political campaigns. My best speeches have been non-political or presentations praising others. My introductions of Dick Lugar, Jim Baker, Mrs. Coretta Scott King, and a few other less public figures have produced more thunderous standing ovations for those persons than those speeches in my own interest. The same is true where I have given speeches substituting for Senator Lugar. So in a campaign, I might be tempted to praise my opponents to my own detriment. When I was executive director, president, or servant of the Bradford, Cleveland, Brooks Institute on the Oakwood University campus, I chaired a national awards program for service in a prominent hotel in St. Louis, Missouri. As chairman, I could praise all participants but reserved my special spot for introducing my friend, Congresswoman Sheila Jackson Lee as the keynote speaker. She is one of those articulate, hard-working members of Congress who deserves praise other members of Congress wish for. Our Mistress of ceremonies Dr. Janice Browne of Nashville, Tennessee, was chosen for her tremendous oratorical skills. She is great at making events great. There was a very special occasion in Lincoln, Nebraska, at the second oldest Rotary Club in the world and one of the largest. I had the pleasure of introducing Dr. Tom Osborn, the head coach for the University of Nebraska's football team. That was the number one college team in the nation and he was loved by all. I stretched that introduction and built upon the excitement of his winning record and other accomplishments until the crowd could hardly wait for me to finish so they could jump to their feet with a tremendous ovation earned by a national hero. When one has a great person to introduce, the job is easier. Tom went on to a great victory in a race for the United States Congress. Some felt, with an introduction like that, he could run for President. It takes more than an introduction but some have been elected with lesser qualifications.

Indianapolis politics developed my appetite for political campaigns and public service so I announced my candidacy for the United States Congress at a noon event on the Federal Court House steps. The noon pedestrian traffic expanded the crowd of friends and supporters. Campaigning was delightful but I lost the election. However, the campaign prepared me for additional leadership opportunities, including leadership roles in the United States government working for the President of the United States. Presidential appointments to leadership roles eventually included National Director of Community Action where I managed operations with staff and offices in each of the ten regional cities. These are Boston, New York, Philadelphia, Atlanta, Chicago, Kansas City, Denver, Dallas, Seattle, and San Francisco. This was truly national leadership, funding and overseeing programs in every state and county of the country. My next presidential appointment was larger still as the budget included billions of dollars again reaching into every city, county, and state of the country. This was as Commissioner for the Administration for Children, Youth and Families along with Chief of the Children's Bureau. This provided a continuous flow of speaking invitations before audiences interested in children, youth, families, government programs, and officials from every level of government.

A very important speech was delivered at the ground-breaking ceremony for the new world headquarters for the General Conference in Silver Spring, Maryland. As an official of the United States Department of State, it was my role to stress the importance of an extraordinary facility for sending a message to religious and governmental leaders and common people in every nation of the world. Those who had to pay for this impressive structure needed to know that this was a wise investment. I articulated that message with every ounce of strength and eloquence I could muster. My most important speeches included those for Senate confirmation hearings, other Congressional hearings, my swearing-in ceremonies, national and international leadership conferences at the State Department, and other key cities of the world on issues facing the world. Statements relating to personal appointments call for more humility while issues challenging the nation, the world, and citizen groups demand more oratory. In Congressional hearings, members of Congress try to look good at the expense of others. Sometimes they have to be reminded that you are there to give them information they do not have so they can better serve their constituents and our country. At the same time, they wish to be seen as those who know it all. I, at times, remind those who "know it all" of a statement by E.G. White: "If you knew much more than you do now, you would be convinced that you know very little." I share that reflecting on the fact that I do not know it all and then I broaden it to include all those present, indicating that is the purpose of fact-finding hearings. They get the message without being insulted and then all present can be a tad more humble.

In my confirmation hearings for the position of Commissioner for the Administration of Children, Youth and Families, Senator Bob Dole was chairman. Senator Lugar introduced me with praise for my qualifications, service, and dedication to the interest of children, youth, and families. I made my brief speech or comments and Senator Patrick Moynihan of New York, the predecessor of Senator Hillary Rodham Clinton, asked the first question in his usual unpredictable manner. He wanted to know why I would accept the top position in an agency that would soon be eliminated by the President of the United States. I stated something to the affect that the information I had received did not lead me to believe that the agency would be eliminated. And that should some parts be eliminated in the future, my interest in the issues affecting the children and families of this country, would lead me to give my dedicated service to protect and enhance all our families as this is essential to maintain the greatness of our country. There had been some suggestions that one program, Head Start, might be removed and turned over to the states but there was no indication that the agency might be eliminated. The agency was not eliminated and Head Start remained with a significant increase in funding. In fact, the funding was increased to a level more than the total of the previous two administrations combined. If we had known much more than we did at that time, we would have been convinced that we knew very little of the future. I did receive supporting votes from all members of the Committee and the entire United States Senate.

Other very important speeches include my more than one thousand speeches, sermons, presentations, and panel discussions around the world promoting and defending religious liberty for all. Too many persons are now in prison, unemployed, under-employed, under-educated or even deceased because of religious discrimination or persecution. These victims are in every country of the world.

My next move by presidential selection was international at the United States Department of State, travelling the world and relating to our diplomatic missions and leaders of the world. My opportunities for service and leadership, therefore, had clearly gone beyond any realistic dreams I or anyone else could have had coming from my childhood, youth, or early manhood. Miracles started early and never stopped. Perseverance was required but others have exercised perseverance and other leadership traits but that is not always enough. Results produced by wise decisions are required.

Several years later, a corporate call as an international vice president in a high-tech company, Highbeam Business Systems, led to my exit from government at the end of 1989. I thought it was finally time for me to say "yes" to a good opportunity in the world of business. My State Department travel, assignments, and exposure to corporate issues had prepared me for this position. This was rewarding for a while but Heaven had another place for my service. Our business sector of the economy was not doing well as government contracting requests were declining and another totally unanticipated door of opportunity opened for me.

The answer to this offer, another opportunity that had never been dreamed, took me to Lincoln, Nebraska, as president and CEO of Christian Record Services. Very few persons dream of spending winters in Lincoln. Christian Record Services is a non-profit, faith-based institution providing educational, inspirational, and recreational services to persons with disabilities, (mostly blind) children, youth, and adults. This was most rewarding and it provided opportunities to meet the challenges of national fund raising. It feels great to see those envelopes come in with sacrificial contributions to brighten the lives of children and adults whose hopes and aspirations have been lowered through no fault of theirs. And then, when one sees those hopes awakened and their aspirations soar with the enriching programs developed in response to compassion, life and lives become more meaningful. We can see this world and its resources are not just for us but for all humanity, including the less fortunate, victims of disabilities, crime, and poverty. This is a tremendous planet, inhabited by some tremendous individuals and institutions. I loved it in Lincoln, serving inspiring persons around this country who could claim excuses of disabilities. But they never give up; they, children and adults, persevere as true champions and heroes.

Another call came from Silver Spring, Maryland, with global opportunities to serve and administrator/minister. I was to serve as vice president of the North American Division of the General Conference of Seventh-day Adventists; as director of public affairs and religious liberty; and as president of the North American Religious Liberty Association. On the executive committee of the General Conference and as a member of the legal affairs committee, I could contribute to a great array of ministries and services impacting the populations of the world. As chairman of the litigation committee for North America, I could have influence with corporate America that others had declined to exercise. I accepted the call, the offer, as all my previous positions had helped prepare me for this opportunity to respond and speak for suffering humankind, those with very few opportunities, victims of disasters, poverty, ignorance, and human rights violations. After ten years, I chose retirement and a move to Huntsville, Alabama. I would continue to work on a limited time basis with more discretionary time for more volunteer service, doing for others what is most rewarding and most beneficial for humanity.

This discretionary lifestyle allowed more service for the NAACP as chairperson of the Communications Committee. I had responsibilities for efforts to increase minority representation in radio, TV, and newspaper organizations. I accepted this challenging assignment because there was clearly a problem of underrepresentation of minorities on air with all the television stations. I have spent time with radio and TV station managers, and the Huntsville Times CEO. All have been courteous and polite, requesting my assistance. I pointed out to them that I could not do their jobs but could assist with ideas and recommendations. They have a problem keeping many persons due to the market being non-competitive with close by markets such as Atlanta, Birmingham, Chattanooga, and Nashville. We pressed and pressured and advised and got them to partner with Oakwood University, Alabama A & M University, and University of Northern Alabama in developing internships and other training programs, and the use of minority journalist organizations nation-wide. The number of African American on-air personalities reached eighteen percent and one of the three major stations has an African American female manager. I deeply appreciate the support and authority extended to me by NAACP President Alice Sams and the entire Huntsville City-Madison County NAACP Branch and the cooperation from the communication departments of Oakwood University and Alabama A & M University.

There were many services I could render to Oakwood University; Oakwood University Church; Bradford, Cleveland, Brooks Institute; South Central Conference; seven different rehabilitation and nursing centers; Community Action Partnership; and Love the Children. But I thought retirement meant mostly rest and recreation. I did purchase a boat and golfing supplies but life requires a balance. There is too much suffering among too many for any to look the other way expecting others to provide relief. And there is too much joy to be found providing joy for others who cannot provide same for themselves. My rehab and visits involving several thousand encouraging contacts per year over the past ten years have benefitted me as much as those with whom I visited individually and in groups. Even though I am no barber, I am pleased that I can provide shaves and haircuts as needed. Other automatic referral phone calls to me on a 24 hour per day availability service are also beneficial for this retired volunteer. Even the few stressful calls which may come late at night and may require a visit and a personal expenditure of funds for food or lodging are not as troubling as some may expect. What does this have to do with leadership? Leaders must be willing to serve and sacrifice.

I was a new member of Mayor Lugar's staff in Indianapolis and was representing him at a community meeting. I opened with a statement of my general understanding of urban problems which needed special attention and some examples of solutions I had seen in some other similar cities. I invited the attendees' input regarding what had been done, could be done, and should be done in their situation. We had a one item health agenda but I was giving them an opportunity to share with me their broad picture before we limited the discussion to health care needs, since many other issues affect community health. I was unknown and the leaders were not sure how committed I was to helping them solve problems. One articulate female stood to point out a list of problems and concerns that had not received sufficient attention in her opinion. I stopped her before she could complete the list. She wished not to be stopped until she saw why I interrupted her. I reached for my brief case, withdrew a legal pad and started taking notes. She was pleased. From that moment, her tone of speech, attitude, and comments along with that of the total group were positive. I insert this encounter only to stress that people want to be recognized and heard. That is a large part of the solution to people and community problems. Too many leaders think it is most important that they be heard but that is least important.

President Eisenhower prayed a prayer that is appropriate for all who seek leadership positions, especially in service to our nation. This public prayer was prayed on January 20, 1953, and is recorded in his presidential papers.

"Almighty God, as we stand here at this moment my future associates in the executive branch of government join me in beseeching that Thou will make full and complete our dedication to the service of the people in this throng, and their fellow citizens everywhere. Give us, we pray, the power to discern clearly right from wrong, and allow all our words and actions to be governed thereby, and by the laws of this land. Especially we pray that our concern shall be for all the people regardless of station, race, or calling. May cooperation be permitted and be the mutual aim of those who, under the concepts of our Constitution, hold to differing political faiths; so that all may work for the good of our beloved country and Thy glory. Amen."

All those worthy of the term "leaders" should pay close attention to the words of this prayer, especially, the words "service" and "cooperation." Too few persons paid from tax-payer funds are willing to serve the citizenry and cooperate with others who are paid from those same funds. If they do not render quality service and do not cooperate with fellow leaders, they are not worthy of the term "leaders" or the compensation they siphon from the payroll.

Teaching and Lecturing

I have taught regular classes and lectured to student groups at elementary, high school, college, and university levels. I have enjoyed each of these invitations and contracts as I sought to tailor my messages to the needs and academic levels of each. For the years I spent in Lincoln, Nebraska, as president of Christian Record Services, I also taught regular evening classes on United States politics and international diplomacy at Union College. This was based largely on my political experience in St. Louis, Indianapolis, Washington, DC, and representing the State Department in capitals around the world and at the United Nations in New York. I have been honored far beyond what I may have deserved in most states of the U.S. and many countries of the world but few have equaled my visit and speech at Suncoast High School in West Palm Beach, Florida. Arranged by a local pastor, Benjamin Browne, the red carpet was rolled out as I was escorted by the city police chief to meet the principal at the entrance of the auditorium where the high school band performed as for the President of the United States. When the principal and I reached the podium and she gave a tremendous introduction, I could not help but rise and speak to the occasion as the drums roared and the students responded with a standing ovation. I must mention that St. Louis University and Jarvis Christian College also exceeded every desire and expectation of any speaker. Many others also had creative and tremendously impressive approaches to preparing an audience and exalting a speaker. These included Alabama State University where I delivered the commencement address. This was very special as I was given a ride to Selma with a tour by Sheyann Webb, the child star in the march from Selma to Montgomery and the ABC TV movie, Selma, Lord Selma. Lectures to students and faculty at Oakwood University, Andrews University, and Loma Linda University were all made very special by very positive student interaction. I shall forever be grateful to all whether mentioned here or not. In addition to the primary purpose of my visit, I could usually insert a plug for diplomatic career opportunities at the Department of State. As a nation, we should honor those who work in the interest of peace, freedom, and prosperity for the world as much as we do those who serve the interest of military preparation. The former lightens the load and protects the interest of the latter and vice versa.

Two memorable international university speeches were the Commencement Address at the Northern Caribbean University in Jamaica and International Day at Butler University in Indianapolis.

Internationally, it is always appropriate to stress the interest and desire for peace, secular freedoms, religious freedom, prosperity, health, and happiness for all peoples everywhere. There are special issues in the Middle East which challenge the minds of world leaders in the search for peace, independent nation states, acceptable borders, national security, and permanent homelands for refugees with equality and justice appropriate for citizens of the world. I have sought at every opportunity to promote these concepts to be accepted and acceptable by every man, woman, and child of the world. Those who desire freedom for themselves deserve such to the extent that they support freedom for all others. Those who desire prosperity for themselves deserve such to the extent that they support prosperity for all others. And those who desire health, happiness, justice, and equality for themselves deserve such to the extent that they support such for all other citizens of the world and endorse the Golden Rule as promoted in various human rights and relationship documents. May God bless Planet Earth, its citizens, and its leaders to this extent.

Chapter Four

POLITICS AND LIFE

Respect the Essentials

Politics is essential to life, your life. It was a part of your entry into this world and will be a part of your departure if you depart by dying. A birth certificate proves that you were born and a death certificate will prove that you died. Politicians are a part of both processes. And between those two events, birth and death, you will not escape other political processes. You will be in the middle of politics if you seek an education in a public or private school which has state certification or approval. Driver license, professional license, housing and building permits and occupancy permits, medical exams and treatments, and law enforcement represent just a few other government and political intrusions into your life. Voter registration, voting, political campaigns, elections, and being sworn into office may also be part of your life if you choose to serve or help someone else serve the public through governmental service.

My early involvement in this aspect of life was as a member of the armed services which is non-partisan at the primary or basic level but is certainly a part of the political process as it is under the command of the President of the United States. He appoints and directs the leadership of the Department of Defense. This is true of all federal departments, civil service, foreign service, military service, forest service, park service, public health service, and the secret service whether it is secret or not. Governors, mayors, county executives, commissioners, and county supervisors are also politicians with the same control over those levels of government. So if you think politics is dirty, it is difficult for any of us to keep clean by steering totally clear of it. And if good people avoid this public service because of the bad people in it, soon, only bad people will make the decisions which should lead the way to what is good and right. Even persons of faith will find it necessary to encounter the political system and can remain clean and uncorrupted if they choose to continue to live a life of integrity, obeying the laws of God and the laws of the people. It is also clear that no institution or large establishment on Planet Earth is totally free of dirt or corruption.

I have been questioned as to how I could work in a political system headed by a president who appeared to have positions different from mine regarding services for the poor and disadvantaged. And some have wondered how Joseph of the Bible could work for the Egyptian government, or Daniel for Babylon, or Esther and Mordecai for Persia. I pray that I can make it clear for you that God does not require us to work only for those who serve Him or believe as we do. If so, most of His followers would have to remain unemployed, self employed, or employed by religious institutions. And even there, there are serious differences of opinions as with happily married couples. In modern times today, if we work for government at any level, like all the other employees including the president, governor, or mayor, we work for the people and are paid with the people's money. Even at the national executive level, we should work to make sure that all employees are representative of all the people and that employees serve the people and the interests of the people.

No government chief executive can have the right to employ only those who look like him or her or think like him or her. The people must demand that government employees represent the people, not a person or a political party. Our leaders fail us when they tell us that we can work for the lower paying jobs but should not be executives receiving the higher pay with the ability to speak up for the people who have no voice. We should not be willing to serve in the army, risking or giving our lives or supporting the taking of life, and not have the right or willingness to serve as Secretary of the Army or Secretary of Defense. Heaven does not require that of us and whoever does require that of us is not speaking for our advancement. Sometimes, it is necessary to enter an organization as "an undercover agent" for the good of all the people. CEOs have discovered that and sometimes enter the organizations they lead as customers or applicants for jobs.

Be All You Can Be

How does one who has the basic qualifications secure one of those executive, highly compensated jobs? Submit an application or resume to the search committee for whomever is in power or seeking election. Google "presidential search committee" or "governor's search committee" or call your local public library for the contact information. Knowledgeable elected officials can assist. The president nominates and the Senate confirms presidential appointments. It is helpful to have someone who is widely respected or who has a valuable relationship with the president's team or the search committee to support your interest with a letter of introduction. It is very helpful if you are known by an insider if you are not an insider. It is not required but is usually helpful if you voted in the primary election in the political party of the top official or if you worked in a party or for a candidate. The election laws allow for the political parties to control the primary elections. The primary election comes first but more persons vote in the general election which gives the final decision. Some states do not have primary elections. They have political caucuses or conventions. The party committees (sometimes with individual delegates selected in the primary elections) have their separate meetings and decide on the nominations. In most states (few exceptions) independent voters cannot vote in primary elections. Each voter must declare himself or herself to be Democrat or Republican unless there is a qualified, certified third party. And in the primary elections, the party officials have access to know who voted in their primary. They can then give some special favors or consideration to those who voted in their primary. The big items or special considerations are jobs and contracts. They cannot check for whom you voted but for which party you voted in that primary. If you voted in that primary and one person in that primary won the presidency in the general election, you are on the winning side and the whole side can share in the victory, including the jobs for the new administration. The American spirit of bipartisanship demands that winners share some of the benefits of winning with some members of the opposition party. Parties do not control general elections and they cannot find out how you voted or for whom or for which party you voted in the general election. The general election is sacred and is not open for the eyes of politicians or the public. You may split votes among both parties or even write in an unlisted name in the general election but all votes generally must be within one party in the primary election.

The politically available national positions or jobs, up to seven thousand, are published in what is called the "Plum Book" or officially, "U.S. Government Policy and Supporting Positions." Listings are by agency, position title, location, appointment type, pay plan and level, tenure and term, and vacancy. This book is published after each presidential election. The Government Printing Office has made it available online. After searching the Plum Book for positions which may be of interest to you, you may submit your resume according to the instructions. Your member of Congress who is a member of the same political party as the president-elect can be of assistance.

There are 450 jobs in the White House with salaries ranging up to $172,000 annually. As may be expected, some are politically sensitive but some are not. The vice president earns $200,000 in salary per year and the president $400,000. Some of the jobs at the White House are Civil Service, some Foreign Service, a few are military, some PAS (Presidential Appointment with Senate Confirmation), some PA (Presidential Appointment without Senate Confirmation), some SES (Senior Executive Service), and some are non-competitive, (Schedules A, B, and C). These are for special categories which cannot be standardized for various reasons such as for persons with unique disabilities, internships of various types, and the politically sensitive. Our former presidents receive annual government support of an average of approximately a million dollars each. This includes a $200,000 pension. They do not all require or request the same. One may receive twice as much as another and there are reasons for receiving more in one's early years and less in the latter years. Should you ever join that distinguished group, you will understand. They deserve special treatment and consideration, however, no one should be too big to fail or too big to go to jail should they break our laws or later be found to have served self illegally instead of the nation. No one's wealth should be multiplied while serving in public office except in unusual circumstances that can stand under FBI investigation and not involving stock manipulation with information unavailable to average citizens.

I cannot overemphasize the importance of protecting one's reputation during young years when it appears no one is interested in it except your mom. Listen to your mom and hopefully, Dad will agree and support her urgings. These words are not only valuable for the young but for every age. There never has been an innocent age group. There is too much good in you for you to let the bad in you mess up your life, break up your family, and blow up your future.

I am told that thousands applied for the first position which I sought. Most applicants were eliminated by security checks and what they included or did not include on their resumes. Party or campaign contributions may help. However, some had given more funds to the campaign than I, as I had not given anything. Some had worked more in the campaign than I, because I had not worked at all in the campaign. The process may take months for some positions before one person's background, support, and other priorities are determined for a given position. I am told that because I had been a candidate for Congress, that my political experience placed me ahead of some others. I had asked the Lord why He had me run for Congress and then allowed me to lose. I got the answer later when I was told that I was selected as United States Commissioner for the Administration of Children, Youth and Families, in part, because I had run a good campaign for Congress which gave me some additional valuable political experience. If we could always see the end from the beginning, we would not question why God allows and disallows and, may not answer at times according to our requests.

I had done almost no work in national political campaigns (except my personal run for Congress) when I received presidential appointments to federal executive positions. And I could not, by law, participate in political campaigns while I was serving in the federal government. I had to resign as a Senate employee when I became a candidate for Congress. There are just a very few government positions where a person can serve and campaign at the same time. The elected official and his or her key staff have some exceptions. Government salaries are for those who serve the people. There are some violations and some minor infractions may be ignored but some have suffered heavy penalties for openly disregarding the Hatch Act. Most of us, like those serving in permanent merit system appointments of the Civil Service, Military Service, and Foreign Service can only benefit the political system by serving the people well. The Hatch Act, a federal law prohibits most work in politics while being paid by government. So if you manage to secure a prestigious position even in the White House, it does not mean that you must be a political worker in a political party or for an elected official. There is enough non-political work serving the public, and the public interest. These officials work for the people, and not for the president. They serve the president only by serving the people and should not engage in politics.

The whole State Department is off-limits for politics. The elected official may get some credit for service to the public as the president gets credit for military accomplishments just as mayors get credit for police successes, snow removal, and medical service in city clinics and hospitals. Political appointees generally serve at the pleasure of their elective appointing official. They should be discrete and avoid doing or saying that which could be used against the elected official. Merit (permanent) Civil Service employees have more leeway with Civil Service protection even with their Hatch restrictions. "Enacted in 1939, the Hatch Act (5 U.S.C.A. 7324) curbs the political activities of employees in federal, state, and local governments. The law's goal is to enforce political neutrality among civil servants: the act prohibits them from holding public office, influencing elections, participating in or managing political campaigns, and exerting Undue Influence on government hiring. Penalties for violations range from warnings to dismissal. The law's restrictions have always been controversial. Critics have long argued that the act violates the First Amendment freedoms of government employees. The U.S. Supreme Court has disagreed, twice upholding the law's constitutionality. Congress has amended the Hatch Act several times since 1939. In 1993, a number of amendments to the act sought to limit the effects of political patronage in federal hiring." (*legal-dictionary. thefreedictionary.com/Hatch+Act*)

This needs to be understood by more in order to maximize our involvement and impact. Persevere, it gets much better. The top level executive positions require appointment by the President and confirmation by the U.S. Senate. At one time, my confirmation was held up because any one Senator on the assigned oversight committee can place a hold on the process and can prevent the confirmation. Senator Ted Kennedy was blocking the confirmation of several, including mine. I was visiting with Congressman Bill Clay of Missouri where I had lived for many years and I mentioned my problem to him. He and I had been very active in the civil rights organizations, Congress of Racial Equality (CORE) and the NAACP and both of us had been president of CORE at different times. He said, "Ted owes me a favor, I will call him and tell him to release your name because you are a friend and a civil rights leader." I was then confirmed by the Senate within two days. I was given a special reception in St. Louis a few weeks later and Congressman Clay, a long time partisan Democrat, attended to show community leaders and officials of St. Louis that I continued to enjoy his support. In political arenas, one can never have too many friends on either side, regardless to what you might hear from the "tea party" activists. Common sense assures us that no one political party has all the good politicians or all the good ideas. Each person must have the intellect and judgment to make wise decisions for himself or herself.

In my positions, I have been able to influence public policy and protect programs for the less fortunate. A national program for teenage unwed parents (Parent Child Centers) was slated for closing down. I participated in a special review of its services and flew to a major conference of child care providers at the Joe Louis Arena in Detroit to announce the results and my decision. The rumor was that the program would be closed down due to budget debates. I was surrounded at the auditorium entrance before I was to speak, and a small elderly African American lady called out, "Commissioner, what are you going to do about those babies?" I stared her eye to eye, searching for the best words without preempting my speech and just said, "Daughter!" She got the message and shouted, "Hallelujah!" and walked away waving her hand in the air. A young reporter turned to the crowd and kept asking, "What did he say; what did he mean?" My code word got through to the elderly Christian lady while bright communication minds were puzzled until I spoke in that massive arena and closed my speech with the commitment to keep the program open, serving those children of children, to a thunderous standing ovation. The program was later closed down but not on my watch!

I was responsible for the multi-billion dollar Head Start program of feeding, educating, and providing health services to poor pre-school children and their parents. Those who thought they had political power had already announced these programs would be shut down in our administration. Instead, the budget was increased to more than the combined funding under the two previous presidents. I do not wish to suggest that politics were not involved. Sometimes the politics may involve Democrats against Republicans and sometimes there are struggles within each party. That was definitely at play sometimes during my service. There was a California network which was determined to exercise more power over any other region or persons from the rest of the country in order to satisfy their agenda regarding budget cuts and their priorities. This is true in every administration and it requires skillful wheeling and dealing and maneuvering. In the Carter Administration, I had a key contact (Cecilia Jockovich) who had been a National Urban Fellow with me at Yale University. I received a copy of the President's budget from her before my United States Senator did and he was quite surprised that my influence reached beyond his at that point. And my contacts with Congresspersons Bill Clay, Sheila Jackson-Lee, and John Conyers, Demorats, were always available. The same was true to a lesser extent of all the Congressional Black Caucus. Congresswoman Rosa DeLauro, Democrat of Connecticut, was one of the strongest critics of President Reagan and his administration but was always protective of me and my efforts and made available to me opportunities to testify on key items of interest to my service. Secretary of Health and Human Services, Richard Schweiker who was followed by Secretary Margaret Heckler, both had disagreements with the Republican California network so I always had their support which strengthened my support with all.

There have always been divisions between political parties and within political parties. But not to the extent we have seen in recent years. Issues of sequestration, Budget Control Act strategies, and debt ceiling showdowns designed to humiliate the country and the president are new and destructive. Reasonable people who love America and Americans can find a way to serve both. Hate crimes or words against the President of the United States must not be encouraged by sane leaders and public voices. One key supporter from the California network in my earlier years, was Maurine Reagan, the President's daughter. She had a great interest in Africa and had thoughts of becoming Assistant Secretary of State for African Affairs. Everyone has an agenda and everyone needs others in the interest of his or her agenda. It works to the interest of all those we wish to serve. Maurine and I had good relations and worked together to help provide medical aid to Africa, making deliveries on official aircraft. She represented the White House and I represented the State Department. She valued my civil rights experience and connections.

When Dan Quayle was a Senator, the military and Pentagon leadership loved him for his accomplishments in their interests even often in cooperation with Senator Kennedy. While at the State Department, I visited NATO Headquarters in Brussels, Belgium and was extended every courtesy and special briefings, in part, because of my congressional links. The commander of NATO had nothing but praise for Senator Quayle and his work with Senator Kennedy in the interest of national defense. Before I left government, Vice President Quayle urged me to stay and become Chairman of the Equal Employment Opportunity Commission. That would have been great with my interests in racial equality and religious freedom but I had another special calling at that time. Secretary Heckler had also wanted me to stay at the Department of Health and Human Services to become Assistant Secretary for that department while she was there. But the California network had another candidate and I was also interested in the State Department offer. Mrs. Heckler later came to the State Department as Ambassador to Ireland where we could maintain relationships. As a child, she had spent some early years in Ireland where she became ill and it was thought by medical specialists that she would not recover. She states, in response to prayer, she recovered. Her faith remained strong and we felt Heavenly influences brought us together. She and I were both speakers on different days at a conference in Dallas. I helped secure her as a speaker as I knew she would be great and she was. Just before she spoke, I gave her a message on an index card suggesting three short statements in her speech. She used two toward the middle and one at the end. She was surprised to receive a tremendous applause for each of the first two and an extended standing ovation for the third. I was also seated at the head table and she came over to talk with me about that before she took her seat. She was impressed and wanted me to confer with her speech writer for future engagements. It just happened that I knew the audience very well and I was willing to share with her points that I knew would excite and endear. This made it easier for me to influence her engagements and gain her support for my initiatives. Relationship building helps all parties achieve their goals which then strengthens the relationship and continues the circle.

Other changes, substantive and symbolic, were needed at the State Department offices in Washington. And we got it done, more minorities at headquarters in Washington and more overseas. I worked closely with John Whitehead, Deputy Secretary. This is the same Whitehead who chaired the 9-11 rebuilding committee, who chaired the United Nations Association, and who was CEO of Goldman Sachs Investments when they started giving those multi-million dollar bonuses. His name is on the Oakwood philanthropy board in the McKee Building. I took The Oakwood University president, Dr. Delbert Baker, to meet him at his offices in New York after he and I left government for the corporate world. He made a contribution to Oakwood during our visit and promised Dr. Baker that he was interested in doing more for Oakwood and other HBCUs in the future. There may have been birds in the bush but Baker walked away with a check in his hand. That was perseverance.

Networking is an essential requirement for succeeding on the national and world stages. Political organizations are good at networking. Former employees in the Reagan Administration reportedly have built one of the strongest and more lasting presidential networks in the interest of politics and business connections. But other former presidents and candidates have done very well also. Many political and non-political organizations could learn from this. It is also good for fund raising with hundreds of multi-millionaires and political experts for every level. They may consist of names of persons who ran presidential campaigns and the total executive branch of government during several presidential terms. Directories are published and distributed to each member each year. Alumni associations whether at the high school or college level serve as great networking organizations. Military, professions, sororities, fraternities, social orders, and many other networks can help individuals connect and excel. All names, present positions, and contact information are often listed. Alphabetical listings and listings by states may be very helpful. Resources are often clearly presented with many names already recognized for extraordinary success, achievements, and financial connections. Special events are organized periodically for face to face meetings and briefings on a variety of subjects. Corporations have been created and expanded right from those directories with common interests during the years in Washington, DC. Each individual in these networks of thousands have other networks providing for multiplied hundreds, yes thousands if not millions, when fully linked, to explore and utilize a world wide web of talent, experience, and resources. Face Book linkages have proven valuable for networking and business successes.

Young aspirants should remember that it never hurts to dream beyond what might be reasonable boundaries. My teenage daughter, Cathleen, attended a State Department reception hosted by the Secretary of State and me and was noticed by one young diplomat as she was privately debating with the Secretary on America's weak response to South African apartheid. The diplomat later asked my daughter if she would like to be the first female secretary of state. She responded, "No, I would rather be the first female president to appoint a female as Secretary of State." (She has not achieved that goal yet but she is a political activist, and a successful lobbyist with other business pursuits.) The young diplomat quickly scooted away to chat with other less intimidating adults. I organized special events periodically at the State Department and brought in major foreign affairs leaders to lecture and inform persons who otherwise would never enter the State Department building. These were followed by first class diplomatic receptions in the historic Benjamin Franklin Reception Room used for honoring heads of state from around the world. Networking took place here also.

All contacts presented possibilities for expanding knowledge, services and successes. While I was still Commissioner for Children, Youth and Families, a pastor contact, Randy Stafford, came to me and said that Oakwood College needed some funding to help solve problems in the community of Huntsville. He stated education was important but was not a cure-all. I told him to send in a proposal. He met with officials at Oakwood and brought to us a proposal to create a new program, Loving Hearts, serving single-parent mothers and their children. All the funds for that kind of program were committed to the big universities, the

Ivy Leagues. I directed my staff to include some HBCU institutions in the group for consideration that year. They said the HBCU institutions could not compete with the giant universities. I told them we had to help them compete or I would not approve any grants to any of the wealthy universities. We had to make diversity happen or it would never have true meaning. To make a long story short, the Oakwood proposal was received and approved. This outstanding program was continued for several years with lessons learned shared with bigger institutions to benefit the nation. These funds continued at the level of hundreds of thousands of dollars per year. I kept in touch with my former associates (network) who monitored the continuation and they assured me that the quality remained high.

Some contacts create additional opportunities for business and economic development. But we should never forget that the more employment opportunities that are developed in any entity, the more other opportunities can be developed therein. This is true of every government or corporate agency. Some government positions below the elected officials are considered political appointees in that they are not a part of the Civil Service selection process. They must meet certain qualifications but they may be selected based additionally on political loyalties. Some at this same level are Civil Service positions and the selectees are forbidden by law from political campaign activities. These include Senior Executive Service and Senior Foreign Service. Foreign Service positions are only for the State Department and the Department of Agriculture.

Schedule A positions are for special assignments that cannot be standardized such as for certain internships. Schedule B positions are also special such as for various types of internships. There are Schedule C positions which are for different levels and may include staff assistants and secretaries to political appointees or elected officials. The political positions are usually terminated when the political administration appointing them is replaced. The non-political or Civil Service positions are career appointees and may remain until retirement if funding remains available and performance remains acceptable. These positions are highly desirable. I received a call from the White House inviting me for such a Senior Executive Service (SES) appointment after I left the State Department for a corporate level executive position. That White House call came at about the same time I was invited to be President of Christian Record Services, a faith-based international organization which paid less than half the salary I would have received as a career Senior Executive. But I declined to even discuss the opportunity because I felt a higher calling to the faith-based ministry.

The larger salary may have great advantages especially when one still has children in college, however, one must be careful not to gain wealth and fame and then lose what is most important. Worldly politics can be filled with pit bulls, wolves, and sharks depending on one's environment. I have been fortunate to work with persons of integrity who allowed me full freedom, for the most part, in exchange for professional, dedicated, selfless, dependable government service.

Service above Politics

My work during my early years kept me out of partisan politics and open campaigning. My move to Indianapolis to work with the mayor of that city, Richard G. Lugar, changed that. Even though there was no campaign at that time, the office was sensitive to the potential effect, positive or negative, of every action or inaction on the political office, administration, and any future plans. My civil rights service and leadership had prepared me for that atmosphere and this was to help prepare me for the United States Senate political atmosphere. Each upward step demands alertness for opportunities to better prepare for the next move. This applied to my work with Senator Lugar, for national service in federal agencies, and for my service at the White House which was collateral during other service. Wherever I served, I could never forget my earlier service which helped prepare me for service at the higher levels. The leadership and public speaking skills developed in church and civil rights responsibilities have been most helpful. This emphasizes the importance of serving in volunteer community and faith-based institutions.

I served on executive committees of Mr. Lugar's campaign for the senate, Bill Hudnut's campaign for mayor, and Steve Goldsmith's campaign for prosecutor. Each candidate won and gave me some credit for helping identify issues and positions of interest in the inner-city, and in general, and in helping recruit supporters among community leaders.

Goldsmith, a young attorney was running against a former congressman and retired judge who referred to himself as the senile and Goldsmith as the juvenile. We never let him or the public forget that and the people, in a major upset, chose the juvenile over the senile. Humor is good but it can backfire. Goldsmith promised to support me if I ran for Congress but when I ran, he stated that was not what he meant. He later became mayor, lost an election for governor, became domestic advisor for President George W. Bush, and later Deputy Mayor of New York. He resigned and left New York under a cloud of personal embarrassment.

Mr. Lugar was also much younger than Senator Vance Hartke and Lugar was known for his intellect as a Rhode Scholar and his ability to answer questions and simplify issues. Hudnut had served in Congress and was a prominent local minister. Hartke called a press conference to criticize me for campaigning against his record while I was an Indianapolis city employee. The question circulating was, "Is he running against Hodges or against Lugar." Mitch Daniels, the Lugar campaign manager, labeled me as the campaign's "secret weapon." Daniels, a very astute political operative, later became Assistant to the President, a corporate president, governor of Indiana, and now president of Purdue University. I learned much from each of those campaigns. I saw in several situations where candidates hurt themselves by being petty instead of substantive. That can happen in any leadership role. Maturity suggests wisdom. Additionally, never accept a job in which you do not think you can do very well and whatever you agree to do, do it very well even if you must work overtime and beyond your pay level. Establish an excellent reputation and remember it is yours to protect. The day may come when you can ride your reputation to the top or it may sink you to the bottom.

Mr. Hudnut wanted me to be appointed Executive Director of the Indianapolis Housing Authority when he became mayor, while Mr. Lugar was between offices and running for the U.S. Senate. The sitting Executive Director was retiring in a few months so I was assigned there as a special assistant to learn all the issues, and to build important community relations before taking over. The sitting director wanted his deputy to replace him, not me. He sought to make it difficult for me to prepare and take over. He said they could not afford a secretary for me. I was to use his secretary so he could know my every move and orchestrate my failure.

I got the city to provide a secretary for me to be selected by me. I spent time with the neighborhood associations and youth groups and had special reports at each Housing Authority Board meeting. I reported problems and my efforts working with neighborhood groups to find solutions to the satisfaction of all. I could have done nothing but it was in my best interest to continue a record of achievement with the community and for the future. I was able to secure city resources from to help meet the needs of all without additional expenses to the Housing Authority. Parks and Recreation Department had special resources available for public housing youth. I was succeeding while ignoring my opposition and the Board members saw my productive positive efforts and his non-productive negative attitude toward me.

At one Board meeting, he, the Executive Director, read a letter from the County Department of Health ordering that the Housing Authority clean up what had become a public garbage dump. It was a health hazard at the end of a street which had been closed to provide for a new highway intersection. This was now Housing Authority property. The health hazard was bad for the community and bad for the city. There had been many complaints and adverse publicity. The director stated this project needed urgent attention and he was recommending that it be given to me as I had a reputation for getting difficult jobs done. The Board agreed. I later asked how I was to secure the necessary equipment and manpower. The director was pleased to tell me they had no equipment, no funds, and no workers available for my use. It was all up to me to get the job done. He wanted to show that I had been overrated.

I met with the director of the city's Department of Public Works and reminded him that whole street had been his department's responsibility before the new highway cut it off. He remembered I had saved his job when the mayor had asked me earlier to investigate problems among the sanitation workers in the Department of Public Works. He asked for a few days to plan and implement a comprehensive solution. A few days later, I was at the spot standing on a bulldozer pointing out the work to be done as newspaper photographers and TV cameras were covering this massive clean-up of a half block long with mountains of debris, fifth, and junk. A convoy of dump trucks was lined up to be loaded by overhead loaders, as bulldozers moved trash around and positioned it for a clean pickup.

This project was seen as good training for equipment operators who seldom got an opportunity to develop and use these skills which were needed more often for emergencies. The Public Works director pulled in the director of Parks and Recreation with heavy equipment and workers. They did a great job to everyone's satisfaction. I had another great report for the Housing Authority Board of Commissioners. What was intended to discredit me became a public credit. The Executive Director became ill with stomach cancer and never recovered. I was offered the job as Executive Director. I declined as Mr. Lugar was now being sworn in as Senator and I chose to accept his offer as a senior member of his staff.

After working behind the scenes in a few political campaigns, I decided to announce my own campaign as a candidate for the United States Congress. Friends and associates had been asking why I didn't do that. All those persons whom I had helped in the various positions which allowed me to serve others made promises of support. I was determined not to sell my soul to get individuals and organizations of power and wealth to support me. I knew if I did that I would not be able to serve those who needed my service most. I wanted to serve those who could not buy influence. I wanted to speak for those who had no voice. I wanted to represent those whose positions had not been consistently represented. There are many thousands of these living in every congressional district. I announced and articulated a platform which immediately drew much support from community leaders, common people, and persons of faith. If I could get as many votes as I had persons saying they were praying for me, I would win. Young people who were not old enough to vote were stapling posters to utility poles and distributing literature. Media representatives were covering all my press conferences. There was good press coverage, radio, TV, and newspaper advertising. Friends in St. Louis organized successful fundraising events.

If I could only mention a few such friends, I would have to mention Victor and Carolyn Stephens, Doris Joyner, Bryan Chapman, Barbara Dotson, and Janet Lewis. They gave leadership, financial support, professional assistance, and wise counsel in the campaign. In other years some assisted in other positions, and in my civil rights service. There were many others, especially my in-laws. My relatives in Maryland, Washington, DC, and North Carolina were most encouraging. I must repeat that my cup overflowed with prayers. That was great. I needed all those. However while my friends were mostly praying, the friends of my opposition were mostly paying. When the votes were counted, I wondered why the prayers did not add up. I later got the answer. The prayers were that His will be done and that was good enough for me. It was clear later that His will was done.

I was offered a national position to direct the office of Congressional Liaison for the Department of Housing and Urban Development (HUD). It sounded great as I had experience as a senior staff person with the United States Senate. I accepted and my wife was pleased. We announced to friends, family, and co-workers that I would be accepting that position. A few days later, I received a call from a senior official at HUD telling me that the offer was withdrawn. What a disappointment! The reason for withdrawing the offer was when they checked with Senator Lugar's office, they were told that I was a key member of the Senator's staff that he would hate to lose me. The HUD officials decided that they did not want to upset the Senator by recruiting me from his staff. A few years later, I was pleased that I was not on that staff as all the top officials were under a cloud of criticism for poor or corrupt management practices. I was very fortunate to have been diverted to other positions. We should not be quick to complain when things do not go our way. It may be for our best good.

I really wanted to be Commissioner for the Administration for Children, Youth and Families. I was interviewed but told that this position required national experience, serving and working with the leadership of every state. I was told, however, that if I were interested, I could take the position of National Director for Community Action. They did add, however, that position was scheduled to be phased out with funding and duties being delegated or block granted to the states. I decided to accept it even though it was only a temporary opportunity. I enjoyed working with community action agencies in every county of the country. I had chaired the Indianapolis community action board of directors and knew the programs and activities fairly well. This position was, however, most educational as I saw the creative approaches being taken nationwide in service to the poor and general communities from every perspective. Social services, community development, political action, community organizing, and economic development were tools which I saw as never before cooperating to change bad to good and incompetence to achievement. But the day came when that agency and its parent, Community Service Administration where I was also deputy director were closed. I was given a temporary position at the Commerce Department while I explored other possibilities. And then I received a call from the Secretary of Health and Human Services while traveling to Indianapolis to be honored in recognition of service and achievement. Then, opportunity broke through opposition and perseverance overpowered defeatism. Secretary Richard Schweiker called, wanting to know if I were still interested in the position of Commissioner for the Administration of Children, Youth and Families. I assured him I was but thought they required someone with national leadership experience. He stated that was correct but in the temporary position of National Director for Community Action, I had met those requirements and could now have the position I always wanted. They had not been able to fill the position as hundreds of others could not be cleared by the various federal investigatory and law enforcement agencies. The position sat there waiting until I could qualify.

I was soon appointed by the President of the United States of America and confirmed by the United States Senate to be the Commissioner for the Administration for Children, Youth and Families; and Chief of the United States Children's Bureau. As the U.S. Attorney General is the top policeman for the country, the Chief of the Children's Bureau is the top social worker. What an honor, coming from where I came from --- a two-room grade school without electricity or running water in rural North Carolina. I was informed that I had edged out the competition with my social service, civil rights, and government experience; and by having run a positive Congressional campaign. Those prayers were answered. His will was done. I reportedly won against thousands and have not stopped winning since.

The Administration on Children, Youth and Families (ACYF) administers the major federal programs that support:

> Social services that promote the positive growth and development of children and youth and their families, early childhood education, including Head Start

Protective services, foster care, and shelter for children and youth in
at-risk situations
Adoption for children with special needs.

These programs provide financial assistance to states, funding and
services to every county in the U.S., community-based organizations,
and academic institutions to provide services, carry out research and
demonstration activities, and undertake training, technical assistance and
information dissemination.

This is the very work I said I wanted to do when I announced my
candidacy for the United States Congress. I managed billions of dollars
positively impacting over two million persons with scores of thousands of
employees, a million parents and children, and thousands of volunteers.
My staff monitored all the schools of social work at the great universities of
our land, making sure they served the underserved. There were critics who
wanted to give the Head Start money to the states and toss the children
out with the bath water instead of perfecting what was already doing a
good job. I urged more follow-through with evaluations and social services
into high school. Effective counseling services in junior high and high
school would help prepare these, and those with similar socio-economic
backgrounds, that do not have essential support systems required for
college.

After two years there, a call from the White House persuaded me to
talk with the State Department about a position with the Secretary of
State having authority, responsibilities, and personnel reaching into every
American Embassy around the world. I eventually accepted. Assurance
of my ability to influence personnel decisions and increase professional
minority and female employment opportunities in the United States and
around the world helped me reach that decision. The international travel and
diplomatic issues sounded attractive also. I had already served in a collateral
position at the White House with the Director of Presidential Personnel,
Helene Von Damm, as the president wanted to increase and expand the
numbers and roles of women and minorities in his administration. He
did not want excuses and wanted the roadblocks removed and processes
expedited. Working in the White House was very special. Sharks, snakes,
and back-stabbers pretending to be executives were not tolerated. People

there, in general, knew what it took to produce quality results and to support team efforts.

While serving at the Department of State as Deputy Assistant Secretary (later classified as Assistant Secretary of State), I pushed initiatives which increased the numbers of women and minority diplomats and promoted more to become ambassadors and senior officers to the dismay of affirmative action opposition. Women, especially married women, were openly discriminated against at the State Department into the seventies. Minorities, in general, are still trying to achieve equality. I visited with our diplomats and officials of other countries on special items or interest to America. Human rights issues were frequently on the agenda. I made trips to South Africa promoting freedom with the media, at American businesses, and at educational institutions. I carried the real American message of freedom instead of the watered-down version. The press and Blacks were extremely supportive of my speeches and interviews. I was interviewed for newspapers in Cape Town and Johannesburg and on a national TV program similar to 60 Minutes in Cape Town. I visited a Black impoverished community near Cape Town and witnessed a taste of violence. Blacks had their checkpoints, screening traffic. I saw a delivery truck get stopped and torched in the street. Oppression breeds a lot of undesirables and violence is just one. A visit with college students and a radio interview in Soweto, a Black township or suburb of Johannesburg, was most delightful, exciting, and rewarding. The same was true regarding a meeting with all employees at the American Embassy in Pretoria. The white ambassador, a nice gentleman and political appointee, had hoped to impress me with their treatment of all minorities, South Africans, and Americans. However, one young Black South African started the ball rolling downhill. I asked how well were they treated and if there was fairness and equality. He stated "no" and promised when they achieved freedom they would push Americans into the sea.

This led to a follow-up visit to Cape Town, Port Elizabeth, and other cities with American businesses. I found and reported back to the Department, the presence of American type racism. I called on the American Chamber of Commerce in South Africa to work for meaningful integrated workforces. I promoted freedom for all, including Nelson Mandela.

I got the support of the Chairman of the Senate Foreign Relations Committee, Senator Richard Lugar, the Assistant to the President for Political Affairs, Mitchell Daniels (until recently served as governor of Indiana and is now President of Purdue University), and Secretary of State George P. Shultz. The Secretary was glad to be in agreement with Senator Lugar who oversaw the budget of the State Department. Senator Lugar, Governor Daniels, and I had worked together for many years when the Senator was mayor of Indianapolis and when he was in the Senate. Senator Lugar upset the White House with his call for increased sanctions against South Africa. Pat Buchanan criticized the Senator suggesting he should not serve as chairman of the Senate Foreign Relations Committee. But this Senator had too much character to be bullied or deterred from fairness. Press coverage in South Africa and the U.S. revealed my support for freedom and the end of apartheid. Embassy personnel always send reports of press coverage back to the State Department. Jet Magazine, December 2, 1985, page 12, Simeon Booker, Washington Bureau Chief reported, "The U.S. State Department's highest ranked Black's visit to South Africa in months gave a gloomy report following that 12 day diplomatic journey. Deputy Assistant Secretary of State Clarence Hodges told superiors 'the country stands at a crossroads with choices of opportunity and catastrophe. The White-ruled government must move over or their fears of caving in will lead to the reality of their going under.' The only Blacks now allowed visas to South Africa are those connected with government, Congress, corporations, or White owned communications companies."

Another headline article, Johannesburg News, by Mike Siluma, 'U.S. Firms in South Africa Must Do More for Blacks' "American Corporations in South Africa should use their influence to help bring about political and social change in South Africa, a top U.S. administration official who is currently on a visit to this country has said. According to Mr. Clarence Hodges, the Deputy Assistant Secretary of State, failure to do this would lead to increased pressure by South African Blacks for the withdrawal of such corporations. Mr. Hodges said South African based American companies must show evidence that they supported a fairer dispensation for blacks. And to accelerate the movement of blacks up the managerial ladder companies would have to adopt a strong attitude against those whites who resist the process.

"When whites refuse to work for blacks you, treat them the same as you would blacks who refuse to work for whites. People have to learn to work together for the benefit of society,' Mr. Hodges said." This is part of a much longer article.

In other countries in Africa, Eastern Europe, Asia, Central America, and South America we gave a message of hope from the U. S. to those serving the less fortunate and the powerless. I knew I could say what needed to be said and promote what America should support and no one would contradict my words. This was what most of our diplomats serving in other countries had wanted to hear, but were often reluctant to say themselves as this was not what Congress and some other leaders were saying.

I got more African American diplomats appointed to South Africa, including the Honorable Edwin Perkins, the first African American ambassador to ever be appointed to that very special embassy. There were those urging that I be that first African American ambassador to South Africa but we needed to do better than that. The racist leaders in South African would have said I was "colored" and not black enough. Perkins is a big, tall ex-college football player who was clearly Black by South African standards and was loved by Black South Africans from day one. He was brilliant, wise, and a career diplomat. He was interviewed on NPR some months ago and explained how he stood tall over those South African leaders as a symbol suggesting their days were numbered. Majority Black rule was on its way.

I took advantage of an opportunity to support some very interesting and historic political campaigns in the U.S. Two very special ones were Jesse Jackson for President and Doug Wilder for Governor of Virginia. My support for the Jackson campaign was largely financial as there was not a "boots on the ground" initiative in Maryland where I lived at that time. I was able to go into Virginia and give some volunteer service for Mr. Wilder, distributing literature and requesting votes. My brother, Leonard, once remarked that, of all the Virginia and Maryland license plates seen in the whole State Department garage, only mine carried a Doug Wilder sticker on the bumper. I am sure others, with negative feelings, noted that mark of distinction but no other comment was ever made to me. Leonard had made a name for himself in research and information analysis at the Library of

Congress and often produced creative ways of gathering information and making that information relevant to everyone.

When out of government service, in Lincoln, Nebraska, I took advantage of some opportunities to serve and be a part of the caucus system of primary selections (elections). This is an unusual system and it afforded me a special educational opportunity. My political expertise was broadened to aid my analysis of national elections. Later, back in Maryland, I worked on a State Senate campaign for Vernon Gray. We lost that one but he was an outstanding candidate. He taught at Bowie State University. I was a retiree when Mr. Obama was campaigning and I supported his candidacy from his first announcement in Springfield, Illinois, on December 10, 2007. I had more time for writing, meeting, and fund raising. His campaign was better than others I have observed in following up and following through. Once you give or serve in any way, the requests for you to do more never stop coming nor slow down. I contributed to a lot of bipartisan campaigns and did a lot of comparisons. The flood of Obama letters and emails seemed to top all others combined. The excitement builds and explodes and confidence spreads like wildfires. He, the First Lady, and the Vice President stay involved, making sure appreciation is spread and that one's suggestions and ideas are heard. Persons who are identified with faith should never forget that they serve God in large part by serving people, people in need. A lot of religions and all politicians could learn a lot about service and putting people in need first, from several previous presidents and other public officials, including President Barack Obama. I have never been wed too closely to one political party. When I lived in St. Louis County, Missouri, and worked in St. Louis City, I worked with the Democrats who controlled the City and primarily with the Republicans who controlled the county. Both parties owe their best to the people needing their services most. Congressman Bill Clay's district covered parts of both the city and county and he had my full support. No one party has all the good or bad candidates. I was surprised to hear a most political public official voice these same sentiments in Indianapolis. I want results for the underserved who need government benefits most and receive the least. For me, people trump politics. My Bible-based religion teaches that.

There is one bit of advice I will give to political leaders and those who are under the spotlight or aspire to have such attention directed at them.

You will have detractors but you will do well not to use your valuable time defending yourself. Your best defense is a good offense, and sometimes, one should just ignore his immature critics. Your friends and supporters can do a better job of defending you to keep you from appearing to brag and exalt yourself. Give credit and exalt your staff and colleagues. They will see that you get ample credit for achievements without self exaltation.

There is one final area under very special politics and that is the National Special Security Event which is a part of Continuity of Government. When you hear these terms used by any United States Government official, listen carefully. Not much will be said but what is said is very important. This relates to major catastrophes and destruction affecting or threatening the governance of our country. This could be a natural disaster, terroristic attack, or war which could cause significant harm and or loss of life of key government officials. This is mentioned when the President meets with all of Congress for the State of the Union etc. and one cabinet member stays away in a secret location just in case a bomb or tornado wipes out our national leadership. It provides for government to continue even if it requires suspension of the U.S. Constitution and loss of key freedoms. Elaborate plans are in place and updated regularly. Even the Constitution provides for its modification and adjustments as may be determined necessary from time to time.

It was Franklin D. Roosevelt who stated on January 20, 1945 as recorded in his presidential papers, "Our Constitution of 1787 was not a perfect instrument; it is not perfect yet. But it provided a firm base upon which all manner of men, of all races and colors and creeds, could build our solid structure of democracy." It provides for changes by which we may live better. As an executive official who was confirmed by the United States Senate, I was a part of the continuity process, and as a part of that process, under certain conditions, I could possibly have moved into any one of the key executive positions up to the presidency with responsibilities to continue our government. Under such conditions, it would be imperative to restore law and order, provide for national defense, and to rebuild essential infrastructures and institutions. We had meetings under a mountain which is called the safest place in the world with the latest in war technology and controls, with communications and decision-making powers to rebuild national essentials. Priorities would be established to protect life, restore transportation systems, banking and commerce, government institutions, police and justice, corrections, mail, health and hospitals, etc. That's all I am saying, and all most citizens need to know is that provisions have been made to save, protect, and continue that which is most important to the United States of America and our citizens. Therefore, no matter what threats some irresponsible foreign leaders or terrorists may make and even if they ever get advanced bombs and missile delivery systems, the U.S. and our citizens will survive and thrive. I do not care to give a lot of thought about it now that I do not have to. My faith and His Word teach me to not fear as I place my trust elsewhere.

There are probabilities of other types of terror and or warfare which we should not ignore. Some may create physical destruction and others may seek to destroy human internal values and interests. These include but are not limited to bio-techno terror, chemo-terror, porno-terror, character terror and warfare, along with cyber and financial warfare.

For those interested in choosing political careers or parties today, more caution and careful study is required than ever before. There is a lack of civility compared to times and leaders of the past such as Jack Kennedy, Andy Young, Howard Baker, John Danforth, Margaret Chase Smith, Everett Dirkson, Shirley Chisholm, Stuart Symington, Bill Clay, Sam Earvin, Richard Lugar, Charles Percy, Walter Fountroy, Thomas Eagleton, Everett Dirksen, Charles Mathias, Jack Kemp, Edward Brooke, and even Ronald Reagan. Politics is not the same! That's why if I were to pursue the presidency, my platform would include such issues as cutting Congress over a period of time to approximately 50 Senators and 250 Representatives with twelve year limits for the Senate and ten years for the House. An important work of Congress should not be finger pointing and placing blame but foresight and prevention of problems instead of hindsight. I would remove the class system and make it easy to move from Civil Service to Foreign Service, and military service. Most military personnel and policemen may be honorable persons and some are heroic but many are dishonest and dishonorable. Therefore we should not claim all are super persons but those who serve should be adequately compensated while serving and in retirement. And any commanding officer who covers sexual crimes should be removed as unfit. We should provide for the care of military and our police persons when they are disabled, without depending on private organizations to beg for them for commission fees. I would also make civil rights violations criminal offences with the possibility of violators being fined and going to prison. With such a big problem regarding gender discrimination in the military, many complaints could be solved by omitting the gender on forms where it is not necessary. First and middle initials are enough with last names and social security numbers. This should include promotions, assignments, awards, and others as may be determined by appropriate review.

We must show that no one is too big to fail or go to jail. And remember, there is too much good in you for you to allow the few weaknesses in you to mess up your life, break up your family, destroy your career, and blow up your future. We should choose the best of whom we wish to become, and work hard at that goal each day. With effective programs, we must save Americans for America. Save our children for the country, and save the people for the planet.

The Importance of Good Press Relations

Politics is a very broad term covering activities seen in many professions and work places. Media entities are very political from endorsing candidates to supporting positions taken by candidates and politicians. When I worked for Senator Lugar, I did much to help individuals, businesses, and various groups to secure jobs and create opportunities for individuals to gain employment. I helped individuals secure government jobs and businesses secure government contracts. I conducted public hearings on issues relating to employment needs of the state. One businessman wanted to expand and increase his businesses. One of his businesses was a limousine service. His clients included entertainers and athletes. He felt he needed a gun permit to provide protection for his clients. Representing, Senator Lugar, I recommended him for consideration for said permit. He had recommendations from the police chief, United States Martial, and community organizations as he was known for community service. Later, a young man sought to break into his limo while he and another were waiting inside for a third person. The young man smashed a heavily tinted window with a brick and started to throw another brick, not seeing the owner seated inside. The owner shot and killed the young man. The dead youth's mother discovered that the limo owner had an old police record and should not have been issued a gun permit. The television program, Sixty Minutes, took up the case and interviewed me on national TV.

I no longer worked for the Senator at the time of the Sixty Minute interview. I was at the U.S. Department of State and was interviewed in the State Department lobby with all the flags representing the international reach and power of the Department serving as background. Before we went on the air, the interviewer, Morley Safer, and I had a very friendly chat making it clear to me that he was not interested in placing any blame on me. However, when the camera was activated, his first question was, "Mr. Hodges, why did you recommend on United States Senate letterhead with the authority of a United States Senator that an ex-convict be given a gun permit?" I sensed some "political" or "gotcha" motivation in the wording and tone of that question. My response necessarily needed to cover the politics of the question so I stated, "In my representation of a United States Senator, I had no authority to check police records. The Police Chief and the United States Martial did have that authority, but the responsibility for checking that record was with the U.S. Alcohol, Tobacco, and Firearms agency (ATF) before they issued the permit." For the Senator, I confirmed that the limo operator was a businessman known in the community as one with integrity and job opportunities for our citizens. I added, "The Senator supports the creation of job opportunities and the expansion of small businesses but it was unconscionable for the ATF to issue such permit with their responsibility and ability to check background records." The interviewer then agreed with all I said and proceeded to place all the blame on ATF with praise for me and Senator Lugar for supporting job opportunities.

I enjoyed the give and take on Sixty Minutes especially since Dr. Sherman Cox told me that I floored the interviewer with the forceful use of one word: "unconscionable" and he never recovered. I was impressed with the approach in a similar interview in Cape Town, South Africa. The interviewer met with me for at least 15 minutes before we went on air. She wanted to make sure I was comfortable with the setting and with her. There was no competition or combat. The goal was to inform the public not defeat the interviewee. There was a lot of unfairness in that country but from my meeting with the press, radio, TV, and newspaper, I appreciated the fairness in my political discussions. I urged democracy and freedom for all people, including Nelson Mandela, in the interest of the whole nation.

C-Span was more substantive when I had an hour to promote all the good that was being done for Head Start and other programs for children and families. An interview followed by questions asked by telephone callers kept the subject matter interesting. Many persons had thought these social programs had been gutted when our budget had actually been increased significantly. My testimonies before Congress were against budget cuts and for increases which would save money, health, and lives. And as I traveled over the country from week to week, the press always wanted to know our plans for children and families. The administration, in general, called for government to do more with less. For children and families, I urged that we do a lot more for a little more. The President indicated no problem with that. The cable networks have brought additional combat to interviews involving political issues. Fox News, MSNBC, and talk radio have brought more divisiveness to American politics. This has hurt the interest in bipartisanship and has lowered the quality of political candidates. Politics now is more about attack and destroy and this may discourage the best and brightest.

After I went to the State Department, the press, primarily outside of Washington, wanted to know from me, the bang we were getting from our diplomatic bucks. Many questioned the need for the U.S. Agency for International Development. Senator Jesse Helms helped generate that interest. Some thought we should cut our charitable programs at home and abroad. Some thought the world was becoming more dependent when all should become more independent. They had not considered some costs for moving food from farms to processing plants to markets convenient to tables where there were no highways. And there had been too little thought given to disasters like floods, droughts, forest fires, and destructive storms in the United States and around the world. Education for the general public is always necessary in a democracy where the people must agree to government spending. The importance of perseverance needs emphasis from every perspective. The press must ask the questions and insist on answers. Politicians must research and be convinced of their positions and support for same in their communities. All public and community entities should persist and persevere in separating political interests from the peoples' interests.

Current negative concepts of American politics: (1) Politics of Hate (Teach multi-perspective unworthiness of opposition to the electorate.); (2) Payback Politics (Get revenge on political parties; do unto others as they do unto you.); (3) Politics of Deception (Mislead at every opportunity; destroy the opposition at any cost.); (4) Politics of Greed (Get rich during your first term of office; reward your supporters at the expense of the people.); (5) Legalized Corruption (Make political contributions the top job priority --- buying candidates by individuals and PACs, and self-selling; make it easy for officials to get insider information for wealth enhancement such as for stock transactions etc.)

The gold mine discovered in the IRS (501 (c)4) Social Welfare political campaign fundraising scheme should be ended and allowed only for social welfare benefits for those who need such for the essentials of life. True welfare reform is needed here for the wealthy politically greedy as was needed in the past for the less fortunate who could do more for themselves. The IRS should require that "social welfare" mean "social welfare." And our U.S. attorneys should enforce such.

Solutions to current political problems: Form a National Council of Political Integrity to include such persons as Dick Lugar, Jimmy Carter, Colon Powell, Warren Buffett, Bill Gates, Sandra Day O'Connor, Barbara Walters, and Oprah Winfrey to promote and reward honesty and that which builds a stronger America. Such a group could provide advice or mediation upon request to end stalemates. It is also time for the nation to form multiple political parties, creating more competition for that which is good and superior.

Faith-based organizations should protect their reputations for being honest and non-political. Hypocrites in churches should be challenged and helped to become people of integrity by their clergy and religious leaders. Very few clergypersons have the courage to correct dishonest politicians. We know most are publicly silent and we have no reason to believe that they have taken strong stands for truth in politics privately. In the sixties most did not have the courage to denounce racism. Members in the pew should hold their leaders to high standards of integrity with people's needs over officials' greed. These failures identify them with Judas and Peter (before the resurrection) and make it difficult for their children to develop strong faith.

Polls show that the general public has very little confidence in the competence and integrity of our elected officials. They too often depend on polls to tell them what to do when they are being paid to figure out what will be best for the country. Their travels around the world and their public hearings with experts from every corner, along with their well-paid professional staffs should place them in a better position to make decisions without many expensive polls being taken. And if their intellectual capabilities are insufficient, perhaps new requirements should be adopted for selecting those with greater intellectual capacities.

Some of our public institutions would be happy to suggest testing and evaluation tools. As a part of major debates, they could be given written assignments during commercial breaks. They could simply draft a quick letter to a citizen with a federal agency problem or a letter to the president of another country or to a U.S. official such as the Federal Reserve Chair. Just a simple letter may reveal some communication skills, general knowledge, or weaknesses beyond public speaking. We keep hearing that government is broken. Perhaps it is our system of selecting government officials that is broken.

We too frequently hear positions stated which seem incongruent coming from one person. It is great to protect the unborn, however, some wish to do that but ignore the born, sick children, unemployed parents, sick grandparents, and those with disabilities. In the health insurance debate, how can health be protected without quality insurance. How can we say it is American to give parents choices to deny their children quality insurance or allow them to use the equivalent of a ponzi policy from Madoff Health Care? Who will pay for their care when Madoff cancels after one month of extraordinary costs? How can we proudly say to ourselves that we have the best health care in the world when millions have no coverage and scores of thousands are dying or surviving long term in conditions they cannot identify as life or death. We know, in many cases, money and insurance can provide better but a lack of compassion overrules in the name of freedom. Perhaps, I should say in the name of politics. I can't help but think there was a time when politics was more about service and a lot less about greed. Latter and vice versa.

Politicians are quick to use religion in seeking success. I have no complaint about such if there is consistency between their words and their actions. Most seem never to have read the words of Jesus calling for His followers to love their enemies. (Matthew 5:44) There is too much hatred displayed toward their political opposition. Candidates should do more to campaign for an office instead of campaigning against others. There is also a need for "Christian candidates" to read what Jesus said about the good Samaritan who cared for an unknown person in need. (Luke 10:30-37) They also need to consider the appeal from Christ for His followers to give and care for persons who are poor without food, clothing, and shelter. (Matthew 25:34-40) Except for the grace of God, we could have been born in less favorable situations and could have enjoyed less favorable health and economic conditions.

There are some decisions we did not make regarding our lives, disabilities, earthquakes, tsunamis, and other catastrophes. We did not choose our family successes and failures. We have not achieved by ourselves. Christians should support those who support the concepts promoted by Christ. Majority religions should be magnanimous toward minority religions. Each should be tolerant and without condemnation of others. This is essential for national unity which is in the best interest of each citizen. The Golden Rule is always operative.

Chapter Five

GIVE DIPLOMACY A CHANCE

There are many instruments for helping make this a better world. We hear more about war but we should give diplomacy a chance before going to extremes or giving up on the humanity in humankind. The same is true with our choices of professions. I urge youth to consider all the attractive careers with tremendous rewards and wealth but before the decision is made, give the various ministries and services careful consideration. Additionally, unless you sense a very special calling to a given service or cause, give diplomacy a thought. Diplomatic professionals are considered generalists as compared to the specialists such as nurses, secretaries, physicians, and diplomatic security. The generalists are divided into four professional groups or cones: political, economic, administrative, and consular. Written and oral exams are a part of acceptance. A person qualifying for one cone can probably qualify for more than one. Grade levels and promotion processes are similar to the military. Those interested in diplomatic careers should go to www.state.gov and search "Foreign Service Exams". All the details are there for your review.

The Secretary of State of the United States is our Chief Diplomat and also, among our government executives, is first in line for the presidency following the Vice President, Speaker of the House, and Senate President Pro Tem. However, under certain catastrophic conditions, these changes and provisions could experience a major shake-up in the interest of national security and the continuity of our government as I have already stated.

During my years at the U.S. Department of State some of my personnel duties involved recruiting diplomats or Foreign Service officers. I was also involved in the training and orientation of both Civil Service and Foreign Service personnel. My office was part of the Secretary's office and I had a staff in that headquarters building with other collateral personnel in each of our embassies around the world. I was involved in the recruitment, evaluation, selection, and promotion processes for diplomats to help insure quality of personnel. I will mention a few human interest situations to help those with an interest in a possible career in the Department. I am not getting involved specifically with international unilateral and multilateral issues as I am primarily dealing with times past. I must give some thought to the United Nations as an important umbrella organization which could have been more effective in the past and should be so in the future. Rules of engagement for the Security Council should be changed. The veto should be limited to two thirds of the member nations, present and voting. The General Assembly decisions should give some weight to the population of member countries such as one additional vote for every one hundred million population. If I were President of the U.S.A., I would reduce the attempts at dictatorship or excessive control which periodically surface at the U.N. as suggested above.

On several trips to Israel, I have always been interested in human rights, ethnic tolerance, the Palestinian refugee issues, and religious freedom for all. I can say briefly that there are serious problems with human suffering while we talk about two states with ample protection for both the Jewish people and the Palestinians. People are dying. The inappropriate sharing of land or the misappropriation of land has refugees living in inhumane conditions. Solutions are not that complicated. The common people can and do live together to some extent. Blood-shed dating back to Old Testament times continues to flow. People with religious interests will always enjoy visits to "the Holy Land." Special sites in and around Jerusalem, temples, mosques, roots of religions, and roots of divisiveness, economic and political issues of the past and present can help peace-makers understand the problems which have defied resolution. Issues about the holocaust, current anti-Semitism signs and verbiage, United Nations resolutions, structural organizations, committee compositions, and land for peace pre-negotiations pose real road blocks to peace and self-determination.

The United States cannot afford to buy peace there or in any part of the world again. However, some agreements could be reached if the effective dates were set far enough in the future so as not to affect the egos of current power brokers or power holders. Security, respect, and the concept of equal treatment and equal opportunity, can move the goal line to a reasonable and achievable distance. I have been there and negotiated economic deals. I have been the recipient of red carpet treatment and hospitality. I have enjoyed visiting the historic sites, even a swim in the clear water of the Dead Sea where one cannot sink, and yet many reasonable goals and ambitions for peace and prosperity cannot float in that region of our world. All the peoples of that region could benefit from a comprehensive peace plan as all have been victimized and continue to be victims to some extent. Equal sacrifice and shared opportunities, If agreed upon, could serve as a foundation in many other situations. However, too many persons have lost and suffered too much in times past to get beyond such for present times. It will take time for older persons to "get over" the past and some never will during their lifetimes. Time will make its contributions to the efforts. Concepts from all administrations reaching back through the past fifty years could provide a starting point to be completed by negotiations, arbitration, and peace-keepers. Satisfaction, tolerance, and democratic unification will come through growing pains and obvious reasonable and limited options.

Brazil is a delightful country and my visits there have been delightful. Rio de Janeiro is a great city with signs of much wealth and much poverty. Visitors are attracted from around the world to nice hotels and beautiful beaches. These present some problems of petty crime. On one visit, in my very nice hotel, I was disturbed during the night by persons knocking at my door to offer dating services or some trying to use keys to enter my room. I ignored all as any appropriate official contact would have been by phone first. Every International city presents international people problems which need protection, legal assistance, health services, and financial or transportation assistance. Brasilia, the capitol city, is a modern planned city which excludes many urban problems. When I was there, Diego Asencio was U.S. ambassador. He is known in diplomatic circles as an

American hero who was abducted and held hostage in Bogota, Columbia, back in the eighties while he was ambassador to Columbia. I stayed at the ambassador's mansion or palace and, more than usual, appreciated the luxuries that exceed those of most ambassador residences. At his 4th of July party, he had over a thousand guests who were fed and entertained to the honor of America, the beautiful. I did give one challenging problem to him. In my visit to the Brazilian Foreign Affairs Building, I saw no dark skinned Brazilians serving in professional roles. When I asked the Brazil officials why, they stated that those citizens, as a group, do not usually pursue higher education and prefer outside jobs. I advised Ambassador Asencio that I could not accept that and that he must make it clear that the United States does not accept that excuse for human rights violations and discrimination. He concurred with me and assured me that he will press that issue appropriately. The United Nations Declaration of Human Rights does not accept such excuses for inequality in employment opportunities.

The great continent of Africa has a lot to see and much to be learned by Americans of every race. Culture, religion, family life, and wild life are important areas for study and observation. I have visited the country of Senegal several times with one place of great interest, Goree Island. I have had the honor of being "chauffeured" on the president's yacht to the island for a special tour. For diplomats and others interested in human relations, there are lessons to be learned about people, freedom, and human equality. This is one place where thousands of slaves were held until they were loaded on ships for their trips to the Americas. Many young African men risked their lives for freedom trying to swim back to the beaches of the free. History says they often fought with sharks until the water was red with their blood. Some made it back victoriously, some with one leg or with other severe injuries. Female rape victims were set free if they were impregnated by white slave traders. Like the holocaust victims, the world of diplomacy should continue to cry aloud, "Never again." I was photographed standing in the door where Blacks were herded through and onto slave ships. That was called the door of no return. I proclaimed in the name of freedom for oppressed peoples around the world, "Never again! Never again!" I committed America to the opposition of oppression wherever it raised its ugly head. May we move up to and live up to that commitment.

I spent a month in Surabaya, Indonesia a few years ago. I was a public speaker, evangelist, for the Quiet Hour International Services, speaking on subjects relating to health, human rights, religious tolerance, and education. Some of these issues are normally off limits in Indonesia, which is the country with the largest Islamic population in the world. There is religious strife there with some restrictions and persecution of Christians. I received a visit one afternoon, at my Sheraton Hotel, from state authorities including a uniform policeman. They wanted to know why I was in their country. I told them for educational, cultural, and tourism interests. They reminded me that I was given a tourist visa and that is what they expected to consume my time. I assured them that I had an interest in tourism but I could not come to such a great and beautiful country with such nice people and do only one thing. I reminded them that I had served as a diplomat and official for my government and had traveled the world and found Indonesia to be one of my favorite countries. I had to drop that "diplomat" hint so they might connect the diplomatic immunity possibility.

Sometimes I carry my Diplomatic Passport though I never present it or seek favors, I may have it in a place where it will be seen by those searching to see my personal items. Some officials are very courteous just knowing of my past official travels and service. My praise for them individually and for their country is always appreciated. My visit from those two officers came to a friendly end.

Each evening just before I spoke to this large audience in a high-rise mall ballroom, there was a health lecture on a specific disease of interest by a local physician. One evening just before I spoke one of my hosts came and sat behind me on the front row of the seating. He said, "Don't look around now but three national officials just entered and are seated in the rear on the right. Be very careful what you say." I advised that, "They should be careful on how they respond to what I say. It is all for their benefit and everyone else present." He said, "Let me remind you that some Christian institutions have been burned recently and some leaders have been killed." I informed him that they should have given me that information before I left the United States. However, I thanked him and promised to be diplomatic.

When I stood to speak, I expressed my appreciation for the warmth and friendliness of the Indonesian people. And that was all true; some are very wealthy and very generous. I stated that as soon as I returned to the United States, I would be sharing with my friends at the State Department, at U.S. Agency for International Development, and the United Nations how much I learned to love Indonesia. I assured all that I would urge the U.S. to support every initiative under consideration for economic development, agricultural cooperation, defense, and trade. They applauded in appreciation and I launched into my speech as planned. Nearing the end, I saw three well-dressed gentlemen rise and exit slightly bent with friendly expressions on their faces. I heard no more from any concerns whether official, community, or religion based.

Most young diplomats look forward to serving in capitols like Paris, London, Moscow, Geneva, and New Deli but all places have something special to offer. On a visit to Poland, my business required that I stay over a weekend. I was offered an auto and driver for all the time I was there to go where I wished. I found Warsaw to be as interesting as Moscow. I was invited to a church service with unlimited transportation by a physician and her husband which included a special lunch in a nice restaurant. It was explained to me that we should eat in a public place because their home was probably bugged. I was then taken to a private boarding academy where I met with the faculty and student body. They gave me a special education which I did not get from our diplomats at the American embassy. I later shared my experience with the ambassador as I was staying at his residence. He was shocked that I could have such interesting contacts within a day or two of my arrival. The same was true in Jakarta, Indonesia. I was sharing with the ambassador there my introduction to special Indonesian foods. I enjoyed a special fruit, darian, which is delicious but smells worse than fish. The ambassador stated some diplomatic officers had spent years there without ever experiencing darian and other unique foods. The issue I wish to emphasize is people. To be a successful diplomat, one must gain entry into the lives and hearts of the people of other lands. Religious persons claim to be ambassadors of God but they often insult or ignore the interests of others pressing only their interest in proselytizing.

There are some depressing places. I was on my way to Venezuela when my trip was interrupted. I was diverted for security reasons to Miami for the weekend and then sent to Guatemala City. I was picked up at the Guatemala airport as usual, only I was rushed straight from the plane to a

bullet-proof limousine with men carrying assault rifles. I wondered what
security problem in Venezuela could have been worse than this. We went
straight to the embassy as it was mid-day and my escorts pointed out to me
bullet holes in the embassy walls and sand bags protecting some windows
and doors. I would have felt more secure at the ambassador's residence but
I was placed in a luxury Westin Hotel with no obvious security. I arrived
in Nigeria once on a plane having trouble and no one was allowed to get
off the plane while heavily armed soldiers marched up and down the aisle
for hours. No food or beverages were served and the air conditioning was
off. There had been a coup a few days earlier and the air was very tense.
On a visit to Nicaragua, I was not surprised by armed military personnel
but was surprised to see so many teenage boys in uniforms carrying assault
weapons without the mature judgment to use such. This was a time when
the United States had a tight squeeze on their economy. A brief visit to
a super market revealed the scarcity of food. The food was spread out to
conceal the appearance of empty shelves. Wherever freedom is scarce,
everything else desirable is in short supply also.

I was staying at a Holliday Inn in Johannesburg and noticed the streets
suddenly filled up with people. Cars could not move. There was no noise,
just people milling around. One truck load of soldiers showed up but they
were out-numbered hundreds to one. Merchants closed the metal shutters
to their windows and whites got off the streets. I went down and took
a short walk to assess the situation. Clearly, a riot was about to erupt. I
decided I should go back to my room just in case I received a telephone
call from home or from anywhere. The police did not do anything as
they could not. Eventually, the people began to disburse on their own.
Peace without fear returned to the satisfaction of merchants and shoppers.
Sometimes, peace will come if we only give it a chance. In Pretoria, I
went for a walk on a Saturday night and dropped in a drug store to make
some small purchases. To my surprise, they did not accept U.S. currency
but offered whatever I wanted as a gift. They thought I was an American
tourist and were not trying to impress me as a government official. This was
during apartheid times when they highly valued friendship with America.

I experienced the same hospitality in Jerusalem. People to people
contacts are most valuable. In Moscow, citizens are much more reserved
and maintain a strict business attitude.

I visited the Vatican and took a look at the humble building known as the American Embassy. Beside our embassy in Saudi Arabia, it would look like a shack. The religious buildings and atmosphere were much more inviting and palatial. But I did want to get some more insight on diplomatic relations between the United States and the Holy See after I took care of some American personnel issues. For personal reasons, I wanted more information on what was behind the press for diplomatic relations between the U.S. and the Holy See. There were no answers forthcoming to these questions. Therefore, I had more questions when I returned to my office than I had when I left Washington. I asked my secretary to secure for me the files of correspondence between the State Department and the White House and the Vatican. She later advised me that those files were classified and not available to her even though she had a top secret clearance. I could pick them up and keep them in my office with certain restrictions. I had to sign a statement indicating that I would not discuss with anyone what I saw unless they had an official need to know. And if I should have a need to take them out of the building, I must promise in writing to destroy them as soon as possible in accordance with NODIS instructions. I did get to see and hold what I wanted which included the process and issues regarding the establishment of diplomatic relations between the United States of America and the Holy See or the Vatican. The president and the pope had personal goals linked to the establishment of diplomatic relations between the two countries as the "Holy See" is considered a country with business separate from the Vatican. Pope John Paul ii and President Reagan had needs for each other's leadership and support. Personal diplomacy between these two and followed up by others, as appropriate, satisfied those bilateral needs. In part, the pope wanted the United States to stop giving funds to Planned Parent Hood and wanted diplomatic relations established between the Holy See and the United States. If the U.S. recognized the Holy See as a major international power, the rest of the world would do the same. President Reagan wanted the pope to use his Polish connections and influence to help bring down the Soviet Union. Communism could no longer hold Eastern Europe together as a super power. The power of diplomacy delivered. I later visited Poland and saw some of those Soviet Union pieces come apart while other pieces came together.

On September 11, 2012 The American diplomatic mission at Benghazi, in Libya, was attacked by a heavily armed group. The attack began during the night at a compound that is meant to protect the consulate building. A second assault in the early morning the next day targeted a nearby CIA annex in a different diplomatic compound. Four people were killed, including U.S. Ambassador J. Christopher Stevens. Ten others were injured. The attack was strongly condemned by the governments of Libya, the United States, and many other countries throughout the world.

Nearly 30 years ago, October 23, 1983, a suicide bomber drove a truck loaded with six tons of TNT down the airport road in Beirut, Lebanon. He sped into the barracks where the U.S. troops from a U.N. peacekeeping mission slept as he detonated a tremendous bomb. The explosion and fire destroyed the building, killing 241 U.S. service members, most of them Marines. In April of that same year, a car bomb exploded at the U.S. Embassy in Beirut, killing 63 persons. President Ronald Reagan withdrew the Americans from Beirut a few months after the October 1983 bombing.

Three decades, two wars with Iraq and one in Afghanistan against the Taliban have caused Congress and most Americans to largely forget the Beirut attacks. But the diplomats at the State Department and the Marine Corps have not forgotten. They cannot forget that their work is demanding and dangerous. Why has Congress shown more concern about the losses suffered in 2012 than those suffered in 1983? One or two senators keep crying we must have closed-door hearings because the American people want to know the details. If their interest is in the American people's desire to know, why have closed-door hearings? They should have open hearings so we can know what they know. How can they second-guess the Benghazi Accountability Review Board co-chaired by Admiral Mike Mullen and Ambassador Thomas Pickering? Pickering is the highest ranking, most acclaimed U.S. diplomat in history, highly praised by President Reagan and other presidents during his long tenure of service in Republican and Democratic administrations? Mullen has top rated military credentials. Pickering stated the Republican's investigation was more interested in politics than truth. These men have more credibility, experience and training in diplomacy, diplomatic facilities, military, and security than all the members of the Congressional committee combined. Is there any connection between obvious Congressional inconsistencies and the declining respect for this branch of government and its leadership? I urge that Congressional committees be relieved of investigations and fact-finding and let these duties be out-sourced to experts with appropriate training and experience. Congress can then be more efficient with prevention in their oversight role and act on the findings and recommendations of experts with non-political or at least, a mixture of bipartisan, non-partisan, and professional credibility. If Congress performed in their over-sight role efficiently, there would be little of no need for all the finger-pointing and calls for investigatory hearings. Prevention of problems would produce more unity, community, and bipartisanship. Speaking of the way Congressional committees do business, U.S. Attorney General Eric Holder said, "It is inappropriate and too consistent with the way in which you conduct yourself as a member of Congress," Holder said. "It is unacceptable. It is shameful." Too many persons believe this to be true. The good news is, it can change. The system of change should not amount to the fox being assigned the duty to devise a plan for protecting chickens. We already need oversight of the overseers who provide oversight.

Diane Dillard, a career Foreign Service Consular Officer, will never forget what happened in Lebanon as that October 1983 day brought out the courage and commitment to country and humankind that was always in her, waiting for the extraordinary opportunity to deny self and serve others. I was at the State Department at that time and one of my duties was to serve on the department's awards committee. We voted to honor her with the highest award given by the department which included $20,000 in cash. With so much blood and flesh and bodies ripped and torn with missing heads and organs and limbs, this woman organized, supervised, and led rescue and recovery efforts. Identification and notification of kin along with appropriate religious ceremonies and national recognition and honors with involvement and coordination of military leaders and national political leaders from Washington were key parts of her work each day for several days. Outstanding service was recognized but not enough for her to become an ambassador, as far as I can determine. She deserved that position regardless of the glass ceiling. There is a second such award which carries a $10,000 cash gift but one cannot get the $10,000 if he or she has received the $20,000. However, there are those who have done less to distinguish themselves and receiving both these awards by receiving the smaller one first.

One high career official received both though during his watch, the new American embassy compound being built in Moscow had enough bugs embedded to render the building totally useless for American sensitive business. These awards are only for career officials who are non-political and serve regardless of presidential politics and changes in administrations. The good old boy network was and remains better at looking out for majority males than minorities and females. During the brief war in Grenada, all the majority Foreign Service Officers received awards for excellent service while none of the African Americans received such recognition. I was told that some of those receiving awards for heroism were hiding under beds for much of the time. I shared this with the fair-minded Inspector General for the department and his response was, "That is unconscionable!" I left before any corrective action was taken and I doubt that any correction happened.

And then, there was the problem with Colonel Muammar Gaddafi, the dictatorial leader of Libya from 1969 to 2011. In April of 1986, President Reagan sent planes to bomb his residences and other targets in which there were 15 Libyan civilian deaths, including one of Gaddafi's young daughters. Forty-five Libyan soldiers and officials were killed and many military targets were destroyed. The very talkative Colonel Gaddafi did not make many public negative speeches or statements regarding the United States after that. He had complained that the wives of his appointed leaders were more manly than their husbands. President Reagan's actions led them all to be less manly with their verbiage after those air raids. This action specifically authorized by the President was reported as the American response to a Berlin, Germany, disco bombing which killed one American soldier and one Turkish female. Other intelligence reports indicated it was more than that which so upset President Reagan. The point is, military messages are not usually sent through diplomatic channels. Military channels are often used because they can be very effective. They are effective against identifiable government properties but less effective against non-identifiable terrorist groups hiding in communities of men, women, children, and the aged.

On one occasion, senior personnel management officials were meeting on the subject of personnel actions and affirmative action. I worked openly and behind closed doors to recruit more, place more in quality positions, promote more, and protect more from unfair treatment. I stated in that meeting that we needed to start with recruitment if we wanted to promote more and eventually retire more from top positions. One high ranking career official with much authority suggested in a crudely worded statement, in the absence of Secretary Shultz, that there was no connection between recruitment, good placement, promotion, and retirement. One would have to be professionally blind to not realize that if you are not recruited, you cannot be placed in a good position or promoted. Recruitment precedes employment, success, and retirement. While progress is good, it will never be good enough until people who are in positions of authority can see the need for diversity, quality, and a strong commitment to overall excellence. Diversity and balance are needed in everything involving policy development, information gathering, intelligence, influence, peace-making, trouble prevention, policing, and management of people. This is true for government, faith-based bodies, and business. And whenever negative comments are entered into one's personnel records, he or she should be notified to allow for a response and defense. Affirmative action has not solved all the inequality problems, but it has helped. Many in the majority ranks have enjoyed an extraordinary edge and do not wish to lose such. It is not necessary for them to give up their prosperity for others to achieve prosperity. It is not necessary for them to compete with more qualified minorities. The economy can grow large enough for all to be prosperous. The economy grows when all are given opportunities to serve, contribute, and help make each city, state, and region successful and good for the nation. This is just as important as a strong Department of Defense. It is especially protective from the inside. We should help our children grow up to love our communities, our institutions, and our country. That is where the creation of businesses, jobs, and wealth come in. Our leaders, political, business, faith, and community need to work together toward that goal. We do not need more bitterness and divisiveness; we need more cooperation and support for what is right for all. Divisiveness feeds doubts and fears, low self-esteem, and a need to blame others for failure. Cooperation, unity, networking, service, preparation, and perseverance avoid failure. Even the mentally ill can be helped and allowed to utilize their talents to benefit themselves and society.

Whole communities are discriminated against and hated because of barriers and divisiveness that promote separation. Internationally, these barriers include oceans and other borders. In the early seventies, there were floods in the State of Missouri which were beyond communities' capabilities to control and limit loss. I had over a hundred employees and over a thousand unemployed persons in public service training positions in the inner-city of St. Louis. Flooding in Southern Missouri affected poor persons who had never associated with the urban poor of St. Louis. My office transported unemployed persons during the week to Southern Missouri to fill sand bags and do whatever was needed to protect homes and small businesses from the flood. On a Sunday afternoon, my church conference president and I visited Southern Missouri to get a first-hand look at the floods. We were stopped by the sheriff. I pointed out to the sheriff that I had sent a bus load of persons there to work on the flooding and I wanted to see the kind of work they had done. He was surprised that I had sent those workers and immediately volunteered to take us on his boat through the streets to see all the devastation. He had nothing but praise for the work those inner-city workers had done for his county. That was a type of diplomacy. It helped to remove walls of misunderstanding and create attitudes of human cooperation and compassion. Community diplomacy and international diplomacy serve the same purposes and help make this a better world. I have been involved in assisting in disaster relief in several situations. When I see reports of wild fires today, I am reminded of my years in military service in the state of Colorado. I was among the military volunteers who went to the mountains to fight fires and protect properties. It was hard work just maneuvering among those hills and trees. But it was rewarding to be a part of serving humanity and possibly saving lives. This helped those citizens to better appreciate military personnel and their attitudes of service. The Civil Rights movement, in a general sense, performed a diplomatic mission for America within America. That movement is appreciated more today than it was when lives were being put at risk and even lost. Divisiveness does not build, it destroys.

The year of 1967 was one of a hot summer with violence in some cities protesting the status of the poor and racial minorities. Dr. King and the

Southern Christian Leadership Conference planned for poor people of all races and others of good will to gather in Washington in 1968 and demand the protection of human rights and to use peaceful means to end war and poverty. The planning began in late 1967 and Dr. King was assassinated in April of 1968 but the plans moved forward with leadership from his assistant, Dr. Ralph Abernathy, and Mrs. Coretta Scott King along with leaders of other civil rights organizations. People started gathering by the thousands in May 1968 and were housed under a large tent called Tent City and Resurrection City. The goal was for $30 billion to provide for an end to poverty with jobs, income, training, and housing. I was there as president of the St. Louis Congress of Racial Equality (CORE) promoting unity within for success without. And that is what is needed now for the United States prosperity and for world peace. This kind of diplomacy, this kind of respect for all humanity, this kind of initiative for global economic development should be our leaders' goals even if it is thought improbable or impossible to achieve. The only thing which can render that goal impossible is greed, group discrimination, and selfishness within individual politicians, corporations, and political parties. In other words, divisiveness fails.

The efforts to end poverty and bring equality among the races have not achieved success. The "New South" is the whole United States. The problems of all states are about equal with their inequalities. There is no migration from one region of the country to another in search of equality as was in much earlier years. There is movement from every region to every region. The concerns expressed for group advancement is generally for the advancement of the middle class and for the "over-taxed" wealthy. The poor are often blamed for their poverty. Compassionate appeals are either middle class-centered or wealthy-centered. The fear often is that children of the wealthy may not enjoy the wealth level of their parents. The claim is that the wealthy will create jobs if their wealth is sufficiently increased. However, the individuals who have received multimillion dollar bonuses from Wall Street have not created any noticeable jobs beyond a few servants for their households. The same is true for Silicon Valley employees, athletes, and entertainers. But not only those; corporate executives who earn a million dollars or more per year do not use those salaries for creating jobs for the unemployed or underemployed. Individual wealth is used to multiply individual wealth. According to the National Memo of March 5, 2013, "The top 1 percent enjoyed 81 percent of all the increased income since 2009. Just over half of the gains went to the top one-tenth of 1 percent, and 39 percent of all the income gains went to the top 1 percent of the top 1 percent. In 2011, the average employee was making $59.00 more than he was making in 1966 while the average individual in the top 10 percent was making $185,000.00 more than he was making in 1966. Who can justify the top 1% enjoying an income increase of 20% per year and the rest of the nation receiving only 1% increase? And if it were not for the rest of the nation working, spending, and supporting the top earners, there would not be these top earners. These figures were adjusted for current dollars and came from an analysis of IRS statistics. Goldman Sachs confirmed these statistics in September of 2013. The point is, the rich is getting very much richer at the expense of the middle class and the poor who do most of the work, build most of the products, and perform most of the services. In the public policy debates, those with power to get things done are calling for the removal of barriers separating them from more wealth but never for the removal of barriers separating the poor from improved health. They want government to remove the barriers for their private education but never remove barriers to give the poor a quality education. They want removal of the barriers which keep employers from firing without cause but never remove the barriers which deny religious freedom in the workplace. They want removal of barriers to gun ownership but not the barriers to the misuse of weapons. They want government to solve their problems (regulations which protect consumers) while agencies serving the middle-class and poor should do less or be defunded. Their call for deregulation is a call to satisfy greed, which cannot be satisfied. Somebody should care.

The income of a single company and its employees had a tremendous affect on the nation's average income per employee in 2012. The federal Bureau of Labor Statistics reported in one week that the average weekly wage in San Mateo County, California rose an astounding 107% from a year earlier to $3,240. That's the equivalent of $168,000 a year, and more than 50% higher than for the next-place finisher, New York Borough Manhattan, which came in at $2,107 a week, or roughly $110,000 a year. Now, that's not bad.

How could this happen? The Labor Department doesn't discuss specific employers, but several indicators suggest Face Book, which is based in Menlo Park, California, part of San Mateo County, had the big individual increases in one week. The county's wage surge was included in a detailed report on employment and wages for each of the nation's more than 3,000 counties, based on reports filed by employers. Within San Mateo County, the industry that most stands out is what the government labels "computer systems design services." According to the Labor Department, the roughly 6,200 workers in San Mateo County in that industry group collected total wages of $6.8 billion in the fourth quarter alone. That's an average of $82,891 a week, or roughly $4.3 million a year. Those were not regular paychecks. The department's definition of "wages" can include bonuses, stock and stock options. Though the extremely larger than average income is not as bad as it appears, it is still tremendous from any perspective. How many persons reading this book have earned or may expect to earn $82,000 in any one week in his or her lifetime? What does it mean from this perspective that all persons are created equal? What is the value of other professions in comparison? Fortunately, income is not the only factor which indicates the value of one's work or service. But that still is not a good indicator of our value system. It is an indictment of said value system and of our systems designed to protect small investors and producers of goods and services. Included in the many changes needed in our tax code are incentives to insure excessive income (individual and corporate) is invested in the growth of the national economy or is taxed for the growth of our national economy. This will provide for education, social services, infrastructure, and national debt elimination. Adequate social services will help solve the problems of violence from the mentally ill. More can also be done to secure weapons from those who should not have access to such. We can pay as we grow. Everyone will benefit as joblessness of the able-bodied and able-minded can begin its exodus from the United States of America.

Some persons, perhaps a few, prefer a war against the poor over the war on poverty. They think holding the minimum wage down benefits the poor. That logic supports cutting the minimum wage as a way of creating jobs. To take that another way, we could reduce the compensation for elected officials and their employees to the average income of all Americans, in order to create jobs. Now we see that could work but it is not a reasonable plan. Neither is it a good plan to deny unemployment compensation in order to force all persons to accept anything that can be called work. Except for the grace of God, whatever negative situation has affected others can befall us. We do not need to turn Americans against America or against other Americans. Our goal is uniting and improving life for all Americans. It is important that all persevere for America and for Americans.

Many Churches Have Lost Interest in the Poor and Oppressed

The same is true within church administrative practices including church employment and salary structures. The wealth gap continues to grow within faith-based organizations. There is no voluntary equal sacrifice among the clergy and between the clergy and the members. They negotiate contracts with the same goals in mind as bankers, when they can. Are there different kinds of greed in the church than in the world? The desire for mega churches has never been proven to be about souls. If so, help fill the smaller churches with those souls. Bishop TD Jakes recently stated, according to The Atlanta Daily World and blackamericaweb.com, he is tired of the Hollywood spirit taking over the church. He believes this spirit has led people to stray away from the purpose of the church. Too many people are focused on the size of the church and the popularity of the minister. (See Speakin' Out News, Huntsville, Alabama, April 23, 2013) What would Dr. King think if he could see in churches what we see or more importantly, what does Christ think as He sees what we see? And He sees the hearts filled with self. There is enough preaching about poverty and against poverty but very few employment and training ministries to lift people out of poverty. I call upon America to give diplomacy a chance; give charity a chance.

"Prayer is a heaven-ordained means of success. Appeals, petitions, entreaties, between man and man move men, and act as a part in controlling the affairs of nations. But prayer moves heaven. That power alone that comes in answer to prayer will make men wise in the wisdom of heaven, and enable them to work in the unity of the Spirit, joined together by the bonds of peace." (Sons and Daughters of God, p. 335 and This Far by Faith, p. 93) The suggestion is that work is to be united with prayer and the Spirit. Faith-based entities can develop employment and training programs for the unemployed.

Chapter Six

DO GOOD IN A BAD WORLD

"The heart of Christ is ever touched with human woe." (E.G. White, Ye Shall Receive Power, Review and Herald Publishing Association)

I am grateful that I learned from my mother and grandmother at an early age the importance of helping and sharing with others. There was a woman who was of great encouragement in my early adult years, Ms. Rebecca Prude, of St. Louis, Missouri. She may have been in her late twenties or early thirties when I was introduced to her. She was reclining on a sofa and that was about all she did each day. At the end of the day, her caretakers would put her to bed and the next day they would get her up and place her on this sofa. I fumbled for words to speak as she could only say a few words. She had a debilitating illness which sapped all her energy. Her muscles never responded to the wishes of her brain. She had multiple sclerosis and could do nothing for herself, not even eat or drink without help. But I enjoyed visiting her. She could listen and I could share with her comforting words of her future when she would be free from her health problems. I could share experiences of others who had been blessed to enjoy some aspects of life while suffering from other perspectives. She enjoyed Bible and other stories of individuals suffering from incurable diseases but were cured. There were others suffering from persecution, poverty, and oppression but were delivered. Ms. Prude could not only listen, she could smile. That smile was a blessing to all others.

There is a song that says: You can smile; when you cannot say a word, you can smile; when you cannot be heard, you can smile. Anytime, anywhere you can smile!

That appeared to be the commitment of Ms. Prude and she never disappointed anyone who crossed her path. I was blessed by that simple but beautiful smile which never allowed her to display a moment of self-pity or negativity. She persevered with positive thinking and with a smile. I must ask myself what is my excuse, when I discover a frown on my face.

As we see terrible things happen in our world, our country, our city, and our community every day, we might be tempted to withdraw from doing the good which is needed. But there is no justification to do that while there are many good reasons for each of us to hold on and do all the good which we can do. We cannot imagine the extent of ugliness and suffering which we would encounter if it were not for the extraordinary efforts of service beyond the call of duty done by many individuals. These are those who could think primarily of themselves, their children, and their grandchildren but instead, think of others and their children.

Please allow me to share with you the experiences of some who have served unselfishly. We should be tired of political leaders complaining about not being able to leave a greater inheritance to their children and grandchildren as they increase their personal wealth while in office. They want to leave tremendous holdings, no debt, for their children and grandchildren without regard for suffering humankind. This is often done by financial loopholes they have created for themselves so they can buy and sell stock with inside information and profit handsomely at great cost to average citizens and stockholders. I repeat what I said earlier, none should be too big to fail or go to jail. It is also true that none is too small to help someone, too poor to give to another, too mistreated to give a word of hope to the hopeless, too rejected and dejected to love again, too much of a failure to achieve greatness, or too much of a victim to help rescue others.

During the few years I lived in Lincoln, Nebraska, I became a good friend of the retired U.S. Senator Carl Curtis. Though he served for 24 years in the Senate, he never acquired the wealth that others acquire during their first and second terms. I was president of Christian Record Services, a non-profit institution serving persons who were blind or had other disabilities which negatively impacted their ability to read and communicate. Mr. Curtis supported this service with contributions and his personal leadership. I taught a course at Union College on international affairs. Every college should have a former diplomat as a faculty member or periodic guest lecturer to expose every student to global issues and opportunities not otherwise encountered. Mr. Curtis gladly gave time to help these youth in my classes better understand issues of government and diplomacy. He was a most unusual public servant not seeking personal wealth. We should have ethics committees not just for evaluating the conduct of those serving in Congress but for those seeking nomination. Why allow citizens to elect crooks and immoral characters to represent, not just their districts or states, but the whole nation? Their salaries and expenses are paid from taxation of all citizens. The present screening and selection process is not good enough.

There are very attractive benefits with the most desirable positions on the various career charts. Travel and encounters with a variety of cultures are important to some, especially those who do not have a growing family. A position in international diplomacy may be perfect for such. The U.S. Department of State can satisfy most desires for travel. A friend of mine, Ambassador Willard Dupree, helped persuade me to accept a position at the State Department. He was assigned as chief of mission to Dhaka, Bangladesh, not long after I arrived. He urged me to visit and take a look at some interesting solutions relating to relationship problems in that region of the world. America always has issues surrounding India, Pakistan, China, and Nepal. Bangladesh also has some economic development and poverty solutions so I decided to go. I was also interested in personnel and family issues.

I asked my staff to give some thought to some possible visits on such a trip to that part of the world and on the way to and from there. I was asked if I wanted to go east from Washington or west. I said whichever is closest or most economical and beneficial. I was told it did not matter because Bangladesh is half way around the world so I could depart east or west and return in either direction. Or I could depart in one direction and just continue in that same direction and circle the globe at the same distance and cost. So I decided I could take in five or six countries and eight or ten cities in twelve to fourteen days and maximize the benefits to my office. Well I did double the crossing of time zones and multiplied the jet lag as I discovered that the world is round. Columbus was right whether you trust the history books or not. I saw some creative approaches to the development of small businesses and securing contracts with U.S. companies. I saw American families making the most of different lifestyles. I saw negotiators looking at ways to bring people together. And I saw how difficult much travel and little sleep can be on the human body. But if we are willing to pay the price, we can help make this a better world.

T. Marshall Kelly is a talented inspirational speaker and singer who has performed and preached around the world. He sings for concerts, churches, funerals, and wherever he can serve others but the lack of compensation never keeps him from serving. He sang for my lecture series in Ghana for little more than expenses. There is nothing wrong with persons being compensated well for their services but there are some who serve sacrificially, others who serve fairly without greed, and still many others who put greed ahead of service. Those who are not available to inspire poor youth for less than $30,000 or $1,000 per speech probably should not be invited even if the fee would be paid by a compassionate sponsor.

For many years, I have given thought of becoming wealthy. There have been many times in which I have seen paths that could have reasonably led to that goal. However, other reasons presented themselves for me to delay that goal and give my attention to helping others or to pursuing solutions to problems which plagued scores, thousands, or millions of individuals first. I assured myself that after those missions, I could then accumulate enough to personally give more help to the less fortunate. That never happened but I was able to help others professionally and manage my limited finances to the extent that I could prioritize efficiently and share my somewhat limited resources as well. Like thousands or millions of others, I could have sacrificed and saved more, given less to charitable causes, and wisely invested more to achieve millionaire status but that achievement was not that important to me. I and my family have gotten more out of life to my satisfaction than I would have gotten by focusing on wealth which, if achieved, might never have been enjoyed. I have discovered it is better to help and serve others when you can without waiting until you can satisfy your need or greed first. There will be enough for our families as we share what we have with the less fortunate families of mankind. We will then be at least doubly gratified, satisfied, and rewarded. I did this informally for years as I encountered persons with unique or urgent needs. As my children grew and began to advance through college or beyond other areas of dependency and significant financial demands, I started a small youth development project in Maryland designed so I could inspire youth to expand and pursue their dreams. Writing and speaking to various groups was sufficient for some and for others awards, plaques, and certificates of achievement and recognition gave them a needed boost. However, others needed a financial stimulus. Sometimes just a few dollars of encouragement would give the message that they were appreciated and that someone had faith in their character and abilities. Many others needed more help with special needs, including scholarships. Sometimes, friends at educational institutions would tell me of students who desperately needed a few hundred dollars from a few different donors in order to get over a big obstacle. I have gladly responded even though many times I never met the students or may not have recorded their names.

One friend, Shirley Iheanacho, who was in an educational administrative position to know such students in need, repeatedly gave me opportunities to assist. She has often returned to me to share reports of their successes which otherwise could not have been achieved. My appeal to others is, do not wait until you can do something big for a person in need. Do what you can. Your personal rewards will come. For many years, I have assisted many youth, many families, and senior citizens with financial and other assistance over walls of discouragement which work against success. House rent, mortgage payments, automobiles, groceries, and other necessities are often denied by governmental agencies and many charitable organizations. Someone should say yes with at least a token of encouragement. I hope to continue this to the extent that I can to the day of my death. I have used and shall use only my personal funds, neither asking nor accepting contributions from others.

There are educational decision-makers who need the vision to do more for those needing educational assistance. Free public education should be available for all our children and youth through 14 years and twenty years of age without counting pre-school for all those needing that. Employers should see the need to provide educational assistance for children of their employees. Congress should see the benefits of providing college loans without interest charges. There is no justification for charging interest for students who are willing to make significant contributions to the betterment of our country by raising the educational level hence the economy and quality of life for the nation. We must save this country, if it is to be saved, from mediocrity, poverty, and antisocial behavior by youth and adults. The youth will be a prominent part of the problem or a prominent part of the solution. Free education through at least two years of college or trade school along with interest-free loans for the upper two years of college and through terminal degrees and special certification will help.

On the subject of stewardship and wealth accumulation, it is most important that individuals and families manage their resources well. In retirement years and years of illnesses and disabilities, we should have saved some for those rainy days. The stock market is no guarantee but it is an excellent source for some investments. There is no guarantee but there are options and opportunities for reasonable expectations. If it sounds too good to be true, avoid it. Seek advice from wise counselors and never put all your investment eggs in the same basket. I have experienced some excellent gains and some losses, with the gains sufficiently exceeding the losses to justify my confidence in the system. However, in the final analysis, we may see the day come when all human systems will fail and crash into the dust. Hold on to your backup plan which is out of this world.

My wife received a traffic summons for speeding in the City of St. Louis, Missouri. She did not want to go to court alone so I went with her and stepped forward when her name was called. The judge, the honorable Nathan Young, leaned forward and asked if I were the Mr. Hodges from the Northside Church. I answered, "Yes, your honor." He began his speech by thanking me for my personal public sacrifice, stating that I give too much service to the City of St. Louis, solving problems of families, youth, adults, men and women to leave my work for a traffic violation. He stated I had made this a better city by providing job opportunities and preparing individuals to be productive members of society and that I should not be spending my valuable time in municipal court. He dismissed the charge and thanked me for being a role model. I did not deserve an ovation from the court but was thankful for my opportunity to serve and be appreciated.

I spent much of the summer of 1973 at Occidental College in Eagle Rock, California, a suburb of Los Angeles, near Glendale, finishing the requirements for my Masters Degree in Urban Studies. I was in my thirties living in the dorm with the type of youth who kept Barack Obama from being a serious student when he was there a few years later. As a mature man with a wife and four children back in Indianapolis, I had no option but to be a serious student. The mayor of Indianapolis was anticipating my soon return to my serious work-load of two demanding jobs. As I was perfecting my thesis one night, I heard the sound of fireworks or gunshots. These sounds were followed by screams but I assumed they were screams of fun. As they continued, I knew that was not fun so I rushed out in the direction of the sounds. I arrived and saw a policeman lying in this short dead-end street. A few residents started gathering as I directed them to call the police as this was before the common usage of cell phones. I assured him that he would be ok as help was on the way. I loosened his collar, placed his hat under his head, tried to make him comfortable, asked what else I could do for him, and prayed for his well-being. The police and emergency medical personnel arrived and did what they were supposed to do.

I was disturbed with residents in apartments on both sides of the street that I would be the only one there to help though I had to run the distance of a full block across the campus lawn not knowing if I too would face a gun and bullets. One gentleman said he saw the shooter and gave the police a description. The description he gave could have matched his description of me. I pointed that out to the detective and told him I did not want any trouble from my being there. I had handled the policeman's hat with my fingerprints on that plastic bib. I was told I had nothing to worry about. The shooting victim was rushed to Glendale Adventist Hospital. I visited there the next day and though I could not see him, he was expected to recover. Every time something bad happens in any community to anyone, there is an opportunity for someone to do good. Sometimes, someone or some persons rise to the demands but too often, everyone waits for someone and no one does what could be done by anyone.

I was leaving my office one day at lunch time and encountered a crowd enjoying a fight. My deputy director, with his insensitivity to poor and unemployed persons, had squared off with another gentleman who grabbed a folding metal chair and charged the deputy. I grabbed the chair man and was holding him from the back around the waste. Another employee who was once a player with the Harlem Globetrotters, therefore big and tall, grabbed me and the chair man with his arms around the two of us. I was sandwiched in the middle, shorter than both. I turned around and stooped as I sought to squeeze out of the middle to my own freedom. The Globetrotter's ballpoint pen in his shirt pocket got caught under my eyelid and ripped the eyelid. My blood stopped what was about to become a mess for the police to handle. I later learned that the reputation of the attacker justified my intervention and my concern for possibly a very serious conclusion. A trip to a hospital emergency room got me a few stitches. There is often a price to be paid for doing good but it must be done.

I received a call on a Saturday about midnight. It was the wife of a friend I had mentored in high school. His years in war had led him to narcotics and violence. The wife felt I was the only one who could calm him down. She said if I did not come, one of them would be dead the next morning. I was there shortly and thought the situation calmed down sufficiently until she mentioned him throwing away their money on drugs. He was 6 feet 5 inches and thin and jumped quickly for a long butcher knife on a countertop. I stepped between the two, holding him while I could do nothing about the knife. By 3:00 am, we agreed I would take her to a friend's house where she would stay until she found a permanent solution. She and I started taking her things to my auto. At the entrance to the door of the apartment building, she went back in and the door locked behind me. I could not get back in and she did not return to the entrance. Finally, another resident of the building came and I entered behind him. I knocked on the door of the angry couple. He answered and said they had made up and she was not going with me. Fortunately, it was Sunday morning and I could sleep a little late. I do not know what might have happened if I had ignored the wife's request to come in the first place. We must assume sometimes that our efforts to help, do made a difference. If the outcome had been as bad as some others have been, I could have had much to regret for years to come had I not gotten involved.

I suppose there is a little police DNA in me. I have had many policemen friends over the years and this has often been beneficial. My brother-in-law, Henry Mitchell, served honorably as a big city police detective for years until he was given an opportunity to serve as a pharmaceutical representative. I have learned much about law on the streets as I have even spent time on patrol and participating in traffic issues, including radar and speed control. A policeman friend, Maurice King, with whom I was ridding encountered his chief. I should not have been in the police vehicle as we had raced at a very high rate of speed through a residential neighborhood on the way to a robbery in progress. I was introduced to the chief as a detective from the St. Louis Police Department. I did not agree to that neither did I address it. I did not feel it necessary for me to get my friend in trouble though I could not participate in that misrepresentation. The chief asked a few friendly questions regarding St. Louis policing that I could address intelligently. It is good to be knowledgeable on issues that affect people and to know what it is to get involved even at some risk. I was called to a large city jail to be a part of a four person team to help end a riot in the jail. The inmates wanted some community leaders whom they could trust to hear their complaints and see what was happening to them. I lived farther out of the city than the other three so I got there after they had gone in. Before I could be taken in, the three were brought out with their heads bloodied. Sometimes, it may pay to be late. I was willing to risk my safety but I breathed a prayer of thanks that I could return home to my family without injury. I was glad that was not my first prayer of that day as I find it very beneficial to pray throughout every day.

My son, Courtney, called me at the office and asked that I come quickly and pick him up from high school. Students were rioting and policemen were beating heads. I rushed out to see what I could do to get my son and stop any unnecessary police violence. I owned a handgun and kept it concealed in the trunk of my auto so my children would never find it and think it was something they could play with or examine. Since I had a permit to carry it, I attached it visibly to my belt and proceeded to investigate inside and outside activities. I had no thought of using a gun but let it be seen as a statement of authority. There was a deputy police chief in charge on the grounds who knew me as the mayor's assistant. Any problem I saw, I asked him to resolve it. I did call the mayor directly and reported that there were no black policemen present and that he should correct that problem immediately. The deputy police chief was injured and had to receive medical attention. Peace was soon restored; I returned to my office; and the handgun was fortunately returned to the trunk of my auto. I later returned my older son, Clarence, to his high school (academy)

35 miles away in the country. He was late, as sometimes happened, and begged me not to stop to purchase gas until my return trip home. Well, I listened to him and got him to his dorm on time but I ran out of gas on a country road returning home. I took the handgun with me as I walked to get gasoline. I walked pass strange places to the nearest service station. I passed an auto salvage yard. It was dark and I heard what sounded like two or more vicious dogs running in my direction. I let them get within several yards before I fired two or three shots into the ground. They were quickly arrested and turned running even faster back to the junk yard. I breathed another prayer of thanks for all things working together for the good of those who love and trust Him.

And speaking of prayer, I am at the end of a special prayer line where people requesting prayer are referred to my cell phone 24/7. It is often thought that retirees have nothing else to do so they can catch up on sleep anytime. Most referrals are at reasonable times but sometimes emergencies are unreasonable and thoughtless. I received another late night call from a person in a cold rain without a place to stay. A religious group had held out hope to her until a late hour. She was diabetic and had been treated at a hospital twice within the past three days. The hotel manager where she had stayed for two nights knew of her sickness and did not want her to die on his property. He also knew she had no money and he was not sure the religious group would pay for another night. I could not get her placed without being present and certainly did not want her to become sick or worse, because all her contacts were heartless and uncaring about poor strangers. I got out of bed, picked her up and found her a hotel room. She was young. Her mother had died the year before and no one seemed to care about her. She receives a disability check and will have some money in a few days. She had not eaten for two days so I took her to the open fast-food place of her choice and paid for her meal that I would not have chosen considering her diabetes and disabling obesity but she was pleased and pleased that someone cared. This is a cruel world and especially so to the disabled and poor. The prayer line does not pay for anything, however, prayer without compassion is not worth very much.

James Gilley, a friend of mine for many years and president of 3ABN Television, once introduced me during an interview to his world audience by saying that I had more awards, plaques, certificates of achievement, keys to cities, honorary citizenships, and proclamations than he has seen anywhere. I am honored by such and do not display all but when friends visit, they want to see that which they have given me for display. We owe that to them and to others who might be challenged or inspired to serve and support more good causes.

In several different states, I have encountered students and families with special needs. And during times of recessions, family needs were much greater than those of individual students. Evictions and foreclosures followed employment terminations. I had launched an initiative entitled Love the Children. I responded through this instrument to the needs of children and of families. I set aside a percentage of all income and added funds which unexpectedly flowed from outside sources. Profits from the sale of books I have authored have also helped me help families maintain homes, prevent mortgage foreclosure, avoid rental eviction, cover auto repairs, donate vehicle transportation, feed the children, and continue their education in many cases. Now that I have retired, these resources and opportunities for me have, understandably, decreased significantly. However, they were sources of great satisfaction when I came to the aid of individuals and families when no other source could be found within the time of emergency need. When a tornado destroyed a third of the homes in my community and damaged the rest, I did not have to move out for my home repairs and I had a generator. I was the self-appointed chaplain going door to door praying for victims and giving some financial assistance to those with special financial needs. I have been blessed with having planned for the ability to assist tornado victims before insurance claims were honored, and assist others with normal and unanticipated expenses such as food, utilities, and out of town travel. I wish to encourage others to respond to such needs. Some are doing this and more. However, the needs require that many others make such plans and investments in humanity. It does require planning and regularly setting aside sacrificial amounts, not chump change dumped in a can or jar. My books were never intended for my personal needs as I have always given away large numbers to students and senior citizens. And since my contributions and ministries do not respond to every type of need, I also contribute to scores of other causes, agencies, and ministries though I never ask others to support mine. Our motivation, hopefully, is not selfish even though, as we give, we also receive. And even with my retirement, the generosity of my children help me to continue my special projects and interests.

I have a friend, Dr. Ted Wilson, President of the Adventist world church, as was his dad, who promotes the distribution of hope-inspiring literature. He is an international servant-leader of faith, hope, and charity. I have purchased hundreds of copies of such books and other publications and personally walked the streets distributing them. That walking is better for my health than the treadmill on a nice day. One publication I like is The Great Hope. As I was distributing literature in one neighborhood which appeared to need some hope, a pit bull dog came toward me barking and jumped up to me with his feet on my clothes. I shoved him and ordered him away. He did not touch me anymore but stayed close to me and followed me for several blocks and back to my automobile. He ran up to every door with me and I could not get him to go home. As I approached a group of fellows, I discovered that pit bull was protecting me from the thought of harm. I returned through that neighborhood a few times later but never saw that dog again. I have concluded that it is good to assist and support good projects and services of others as I have done for many years.

I have met young adults now helping others because I have on occasions helped them. This includes physicians, lawyers, teachers, ministers, and citizen heroes who sacrifice to serve. I wish I had known fully, decades ago what I know now about the importance of small gifts to children, adults, and families. If we only do what we can when we can as we can, human suffering can be reduced, minds can be expanded, futures can be brightened, successes can be multiplied, and lives can be saved. One of the books I authored for Christians gives much information to help those who want to serve others consider many creative and rewarding options. Large financial reserves are not necessary for us to assist and serve others. Even as we give sacrificially to help others financially, our resources are multiplied for the continuation of sharing with others less fortunate. One of the rewarding options I have chosen is to visit several (up to seven) nursing and rehabilitation centers each week. As a retiree, it is easier for me to do that than it is for others with jobs even though I did much of this while employed full time. These visits include giving some time to some individuals and meeting with some larger groups from 50 to 80 or so. Just to let them know you care about them along with an inspirational thought is important. Their enjoyment and appreciation is a great source of honor and pleasure for me.

I was attending an afternoon youth meeting and noticed a flat tire on a lady's automobile. Mrs. Newman was a widow with three young children. The children could not change the tire so I asked her for her keys. She was shocked to tears to see me take off my jacket and change that tire with a white shirt on. My wife and I sought to encourage that family in other ways. Today, two of her children are practicing physicians and one married a physician. The third is also serving others professionally. We did not tell them how to serve and give back; we tried to show them and they learned from many others in that little church of love called Brinklow. They learned to persevere.

Young Mr. Kelly was raised by a single mom and later with a step father. He and several others were always attracted to me and my youth ministry and service. They were all great but I wish to share some of his experiences. I taught him and several others to drive or allowed them to use one of my autos. Automobiles are important to young fellows. He entered the army as a medic and returned from Viet Nam in good health. We met and he seemed a bit troubled. I enquired and he shared that while in Nam, he and a combat soldier friend agreed that they would always look out for each other. They would protect each other from any enemy and would never leave each other in trouble. They enjoyed good days and bad days and at times stared death in the eye. Kelly's tour ended, they said good bye, Kelly checked out, and rushed to board his plane back to the U.S. As he was boarding, he received word that his friend had been killed in action. I knew Kelly well and he was always tough, never fearful. But I knew he must have cried like a baby as he had never done before. He wished he had been there even though he knew, he might have died also. He felt that he would have given more to save his friend than anyone else. He would have given his life. It was my lot to encourage him. He had come to see me about a car among other things.

I gave him the keys to the car and told him he could take care of the price when he could. He then told me he needed a credit card for gasoline as he drove to his last military assignment for discharge. I gave him a credit card. With the keys and credit card, he felt a lot better. It feels good to make someone else feel better. When I received the credit card bill, it showed the purchase of a new set of tires. When he returned, I asked about the tires. He assured me that he would take care of all that and he did. He needed a job, I gave him one. A few years later, I lived in Indianapolis and he called stating he needed another job. I called the newly elected county prosecutor to congratulate him for his victory. He thanked me for having helped his campaign and asked what he could do for me. I told him my friend needed a job and would do well as chief of security for the county prosecutor. A few days later, Mr. Kelly started on that job. I was reminded of all this not long ago, when a gentleman told me he needed a car and he knew I had an extra one. He told me of his exciting plans to work with college youth on a project to help them pay tuition and stay in school. We agreed on a price for the car; I gave him the keys and title and he promised to start paying soon. A few days later, he called me and said one of the students was learning to drive a stick shift and burned out the clutch. He wanted me to have the clutch fixed and I did. He encountered other problems with his health and the auto. He died. I could not bother his young wife about that car or money. There are times when one wins and when one loses. We came into this world with nothing and all that we have was given to us directly or indirectly. When we lose, One overall covers it for us. It has happened before. Thousands have been stolen or taken by deceit but they were the losers.

A young lady will be a physician in a few years. I heard another family had taken her in when she could not pay dormitory fees but she had no food. I asked her to meet me at the financial office to talk with a counselor. We met and I pressed upon the counselor the need for compassion. He told me I could show the compassion by giving him my debit card authorizing a charge of hundreds of dollars and he would give her a meal card. I gave him the debit card. He gave her the meal card and another person was very happy, praising her Lord. If we persist, the solution will come and a smile will flash across some faces. She could have given up but she persevered.

After my service with the U.S. Department of State, I was traveling to a foreign country as a regular civilian. I waited in lines like everyone else and watched my things being searched, set aside, and delayed. Another traveler went through the process without delay and told me if I gave tips to the checkers, they would move me through rapidly. And so it worked. Agents would take money openly and even a uniformed policemen said,

"Wait, where is mine?" This would have been illegal in most countries but it had become commonplace there. It happens under the table in other places though it is illegal. It happens in the United States where it is illegal and severe penalties may be dispensed.

Trust the system most times but crooks, never. Some lessons are learned in childhood from crooks who should not be trusted. Children are rewarded for illegal and destructive behavior. Many have learned to accept child abuse for petty rewards. Later they accept falsely reduced prices by cashiers for other rewards, warning traffic tickets, padded time sheets, free auto repairs, government payments and benefits for which they are not eligible for various types of bribes from cash to other human services. They may excuse their illegal behavior by explaining how the system is crooked with undeserved persons getting wealthy at their expense. This practice is always a gamble and we may deceive ourselves by thinking we can win. The system is monitored and audited and is usually trustworthy. However, crooks are not worthy of your trust. Their scheme is to win your trust in order to use that trust to their advantage. A friend of mine introduced me to a friend of hers who was a business woman in a distant city. This business woman wanted to be helpful to me but I did not need her help. She had thoughts of doing good to help the less advantaged. I appreciated her desire to do good but she did not need me for her charity. She called on one occasion to tell me that our mutual friend had a serious financial problem but did not want me to know about it. This do-gooder business woman was going to our friend's rescue. She was raising $10,000 and needed just another $2700. She was willing to personally repay that to me within two weeks if I could send it to her immediately and our friend would be saved from an embarrassing and disastrous situation. If there was a loss, she would be willing to cover that but she expected the whole amount to be repaid eventually by our dear friend. I knew I could trust my old friend more than I could the new. I discreetly questioned my old friend and learned enough for me to raise the scheme to her. It was just that, a scheme and a scam. I later checked with another friend who knew the business woman and he confirmed her reputation as a crook. Trust but confirm when dealing with persons who want you to have secret transactions with them. Spouses or other good honest friends can help save you from embarrassing and disastrous situations.

I have been blessed to know the Davis family for many years. Mrs. Davis taught my daughter (who has been a dentist now for twenty years). Mr. Davis was a school principal but passed unexpectedly several years ago. The next year, their son, Edwin, was injured in an auto accident and never walked or talked again. He lived in that condition for seven years. This mother and her two daughters were super family members caring for this son and brother. Mrs. Davis continued to teach while one daughter worked also until she married and moved away. The son was frequently hospitalized and required much very special attention and care but they gave it. There was some assistance but never enough, even with some relatives periodically visiting for several days from other states. I usually visited that son on a weekly basis. They told me that he would recognize my voice before I entered his room. I often prayed for him and talked to him about the things we were going to do when he was able to walk again. I was able to make some small contributions to their many special needs. Simple items or activities such as: baby blessings for grandchildren, play equipment for visiting grandchildren, lawn equipment, special furniture, air conditioning and other electrical repairs, and an outdoor shed. I mention these because of her request for a simple shed. This was important to her. She had recently moved and did not have enough storage space. The garage, closets, and all other space was in use. She used a tarp to cover some boxes on her patio. I took her to the large hardware and home improvement center and she selected the shed which would meet her needs. They came only in a box and the store had no provisions for assembling. It was loaded on a friend's pickup truck and delivered.

I began making contacts to get it assembled and up before it rained. A week passed and all my contacts with building skills who help people in need said they did not assemble sheds. Two weeks passed with no rain and no assembly. Three weeks passed with no volunteers but with a hard rain which lasted for days. I was ready to return the shed for a refund but the rain destroyed the containers which were required for return. There was a lesson in this experience somewhere, perhaps about doing things while the opportunities exist. The sad thing is that this family with so many hardships, lost many valuables which could not be easily replaced such as books, photographs, music, small appliances, and some clothes. Where were the people who believed in serving others? I had spread the need through an international network of thousands. Mrs. Davis and daughters were never discouraged. Others, including physicians of international status, ignored her appeal for a little advice and counsel. A few days later, I was seated in church and a gentleman entered and sat directly in front of me. I remembered he had been the head deacon and owns an auto repair shop with several employees. I leaned forward, greeted him, and told him what I needed. His reply was, "I know where she lives and I can take care of that shed next week." A young engineer, Jason, joined with him and the job was done without further delay. The lesson here was, there are still good people doing good in this cursed world. Others also assisted sacrificially. For seven years we pursued various avenues for medical help which could improve Edwin's quality of life. He held on as long as he could see a promise of help and hope. Finally, there were no new promises. Without saying goodbye, he let go and entered his final nap. He knew it would be short and his family would soon experience a great family reunion which would include him and his dad. He was strong. For seven years, he taught perseverance. Our characters and compassion are tested when we are brought in contact with others who desperately need our love and assistance. Special efforts should be made to pass those tests of character.

My granddaughter, Kiana, is an example which Ican never overlook. She has been somewhat limited by a disability since age 15. She has been hospitalized multiple times each quarter for the past several years. During her time in Children's Hospital, she visits children, reads stories, and helps with homework. As a high school senior, she was awarded a significant award as the second place winner of the Kiwanis Abe Lincoln Scholarship. The Kiwanis Abe Lincoln Scholarship is designed to reward a student for a history of overcoming adversity, as evidenced by an unconquerable human spirit demonstrated in his/her life. She continued to serve while in and out of the hospital through Bachelors, Masters, and Ph.D. degrees from Purdue University. She now is a post doctoral fellow in the Department of Pediatrics at the University of Minnesota researching the transition to adulthood among youth with special healthcare needs. She is committed to assisting youth with disabilities in their transition, physically, socially, and medically into productive adults. I met her physician when she received her high school award and scholarship some years ago. Kiana was interviewed on television during the awards dinner and was asked the source of her inspiration. She identified her mother, her physician, and her grandfather. The physician, Dr. Suzanne Bowyer stated that Kiana was the source of her inspiration. This white rheumatologist was always there for Kiana at graduation times and other special programs. On one occasion, she informed Kiana that she (the physician) was terminally ill but would attend Kiana's Ph.D. graduation if possible. She could not attend the graduation on May 13, 2012, however, Kiana did speak at Dr. Bowyer's memorial service, a few days later, on May 19, 2012. How many patients enjoy that kind of relationship with their physicians? What a courageous granddaughter! She keeps in touch with her physician's family, encouraging them during their period of grief. At times, she struggles to breathe with a partially paralyzed diaphragm. Her medical co-pay for breathing is $200 per month. But with mechanical help, she breathes and loves and she serves with love. She has founded a non-profit organization to serve youth with certain disabilities, The Childhood-Onset Lupus Education and Research Foundation, www.childhoodlupus.org. She understands the meaning of the words, compassion, service and PERSEVERE.

Chapter Seven

FAITH-BASED SERVICE
WITH REWARDS
OUT OF THIS WORLD

I was preparing to take a seven-week break from the Washington, DC area and from the pressurized world of business for a working vacation in Ghana, West Africa. I received a call from President Paul Monk, of Central States Conference of Kansas City, Kansas. He was a key member of the Board of Directors for Christian Record Services in Lincoln, Nebraska. He wanted me to submit my resume for consideration of President of Christian Record Services (CRS). He told me he wanted to test that Board to see how they would react. There had never been a minority president during the 100 year history of CRS. As a friend, I sent Paul the resume and continued my preparation for Africa. Paul called the next day and informed me that the Board was inviting me to serve as President. They had not seen or interviewed me and now I had to make that decision to accept or reject the offer. My wife asked if I would even consider a move to Lincoln, Nebraska. I said we should at least pray about the possibility. The next day, we agreed the answer was yes. I never saw my friend, Paul Monk again. His health did not permit him to attend my first board meeting as president of CRS. I attended his funeral a few months later. He fought a great fight. He was always known for his perseverance. That's how I got that Chief Executive Officer job with only a resume. His daughter, Attorney Carmella Monk

Crawford, is now editor of Message magazine, a position Paul had many years ago. She is doing a great job because she also perseveres.

In Ghana West Africa, I was to teach, preach, evangelize and inspire youth and adults to become all they can become, serving with love and loving to serve, with God first and others equal with self. Three weeks were to be spent in the city of Kumasi and three weeks in the capitol city of Accra. I was a part of the W.C. Scales Real Truth campaign. There were three teams headed by W.C. Scales, Jr., Tim Lewis, and me working three different areas of each of the two cities. I was pleasantly surprised by those hospitable and thoughtful people of Ghana. The surprise came in Kumasi when they named an elementary school in my honor, The Clarence E Hodges School. Evangelist Scales is a tremendous leader and a delightful person to work with. We worked together in several international and national programs with much success. All was going extremely well in Accra until the last two weeks when I got sick with what was thought to be malaria. Based on that assumption, I was given a heavy dose of anti-malaria medicine. It was later determined that I never had malaria and I was given what could have been a fatal overdose of malaria medicine.

It so happened that the ambassador to Ghana had been a friend of mine when I was at the State Department. I got an appointment to take our group to the American Embassy for a tour and special briefing on international issues. As soon as I walked into the ambassador's office, he said, "Clarence, you are sick." We had not seen each other for two years but I had lost so much weight during the week in which I had been sick, it was obvious to him that I was sick. He called the embassy clinic immediately and ordered that I be seen and treated even though I was no longer a government official as was required for medical service. He said I should stay in bed for the next seven days. Well, my mission could not spare me. I could stay in bed during the day but I was needed each evening for my lecture and sermon. My assistant, Terry Johnson and I were such a team that we needed each other. T. Marshall Kelly had been there assisting with his voice, wisdom, and music and could have taken over for me but he had returned home. Terry had too much to do to cover my assignment also so I would get out of bed every evening and take that long bumpy ride to my assignment. When Terry Johnson presented me each night as the speaker from the United States of America, there was a group of possibly

20 or more youth who would welcome me with shouts of Hodges, Hodges, Hodges, Hodges. Terry would bring them to life and they would bring me back to life. When I would stand, my strength would return long enough for me to speak and I would return to my room and bed without the audience knowing I was not well. Sharon Whaley (Perguson) would have a bowl of hot soup ready for me which would get me through another night. On our last night, there was a hard rain, our only rain. I stayed around longer than usual visiting with our new friends and watching the men get chairs and equipment ready for removal. When we left in the rain and traveled about a half mile to our turning intersection, we met a big surprise. Those youth were waiting in the rain for one last chant, "Hodges, Hodges, Hodges, Hodges." Did I need that send off! I was blessed with renewed strength for that long trip back to America. I had been losing a pound every day but the day came when we boarded that Boeing 747 jet and landed back at Washington Dulles International Airport.

My wife was there to pick me up and I could praise the Lord for success and traveling mercies. This was the first of several such national and international experiences of taking programs of health, education, ministry of teaching, preaching, and evangelizing to foreign countries and U.S. communities in need of inspiration and aspiration. Other places of such major initiatives of multiple week comprehensive services included India, Indonesia, South Africa, Greater Kansas City, and metropolitan Minneapolis.

My work that took me to Lincoln, Nebraska, was, as I stated, the presidency of Christian Record Services (CRS). This is a publishing non-profit service, providing large print publications, Braille, and audio tapes. This was a major comprehensive program providing free inspirational, educational, and recreational services without regard for religious affiliation or non-affiliation. The publication, distribution, and circulation of books, magazines, and newsletters helped supplement inspirational and educational programs of states and local communities for those with disabilities which affected their reading. These disabilities included blindness, the inability to hold a book or magazine and some other special appropriate limitations encountered. The recreational services provided summer and winter camps for children, youth, and adults. Children with disabilities need the same opportunities taken for granted for children in general such as horse-back ridding, swimming, jet-skiing, snow skiing, snow mobiles, arts and crafts, and other fun, camping out in nature. This is a tremendous service which should be supported by all those who love children and who have compassion for the less fortunate. Our plant and offices covered almost a square block and our employees totaled approximately 150 caring workers with outstanding talents. There were those who provided social and support services for those with disabilities. They served at our summer and winter camps where these challenged youth loved such activities as skiing, snowmobiling, jet-skiing, horseback riding, swimming, boating, and much more. They also helped educate the general public on the special needs of some of our citizens and did some fund-raising.

Our 150 employees produced and packaged recordings, e-books, operated and maintained printing and binding machines, vehicles, shop, offices, and a host of other duties. I had no great desire to raise money but there was a great structure for that. We had special campaigns which were successful and we added fun to the work. I called on major donors and enjoyed picking up the big checks.

One of my most memorable contacts was the McKee Baking Company in Tennessee. This is often known as the Little Debbie Snack Food Company. It is the largest snack food company in the country with three major centers located in Virginia, Arkansas, and the headquarters near Chattanooga, in Collegedale. The founding owner, O.D. McKee became a good friend. He was now an older gentleman and his son, Ellsworth was president and CEO. O.D. read an article I had written about last-day events for Planet Earth and troubles presented in the book of Daniel. He wanted me to come to Collegedale and speak at the McDonald Road "mega" Church on that subject. I accepted an invitation and spent a weekend in Collegedale. I visited the O.D. McKee home and they were most hospitable. He first invited me to sit and take off my shoes. He wanted me to relax with his foot massager taking away the stress of the day. I spoke twice at McDonald Road Church and after my first presentation, he and his wife presented me with a very nice check for Christian Record Services.

We enjoyed lunch together and afterward, his wife asked if I had looked at the check that was given to me. Naturally, I had checked it out as soon as they turned their backs. I informed her that I had glanced at it before putting it away and was most appreciative of such a generous contribution. She asked me to give it back to her which I did reluctantly. She then said she and her husband thought it was too small and she had another check for me. This one was three times larger.

There was a book written about the family, "Sweet Success," which I had read and recorded it in our recording studio for the youth and adults with disabilities who are served by us. I, therefore, knew much about the whole family. O.D. had a reading impairment, dyslexia, and could not read as a child. The young family was poor, living in a house with a dirt floor. He grew that business from a small investment to a tremendous success. I later got to know Ellsworth and Deborah, Little Debbie. In all my positions where I needed to raise some funds, I could count on a significant contribution from the McKees. They had been a regular family with ups and downs, difficulties and challenges with faith in God and compassionate hearts. One big factor contributing to all this success, according to O.D., was his visual or reading impairment which required hard work and perseverance for whatever he did. And each successful step increased his faith for the next challenge. It was clear to me that the University of Adversity and perseverance had produced another great success or series of successes.

Working with children and youth is always exciting and fun. Working with persons who have impairments but refuse to consider themselves as disabled is always inspiring and delightful. Working with both those groups multiplies the joys and rewards experienced with any one group. I must say it is humbling to fall going down ski slopes in Colorado and watching blind youth ski gracefully pass while you are struggling to get back on your feet.

Lincoln turned out to be a tremendous city to be enjoyed in summer and winter. The mayor, representing a special power group, asked me to chair the civic leadership council which included civic, business, and political leaders. We were always pursuing ways to improve the quality of life for all. It was amazing to see a city of 200,000 persons and never see a boarded-up or unsightly building. The Honorable Mike Johanns was mayor while I was there. He and his wife were very supportive of our services and participated in many of our events. He invited me to serve the city of Lincoln on the Human Rights Commission and the commissioners elected me to serve as chairman. This presented challenging opportunities even greater than my civil rights leadership in St. Louis as President of CORE. The other commissioners were excited about the opportunities I envisioned. We could improve the quality of life for many citizens. The previous chairperson was disappointed that she was not reelected as chair. She was afraid of my goals for change. I pressed the Chamber of Commerce to get on board for changes that could make a difference in the lives of low and middle income citizens. I pressed the banking industry to display more sensitivity and thoughtfulness. One female bank president stood up in opposition but she was wrong in projecting what I had not said. The mayor was on board with me and the Commission. I enjoyed that service and the mayor had asked me to serve in another leadership role but I accepted another position in Silver Spring, Maryland instead. The mayor was a great young leader who went on to become governor of Nebraska, U.S. Secretary of Agriculture, and finally U.S. Senator. I had not dreamed of leaving Lincoln but there comes a time when personal interests are overruled by higher interests.

This call to Maryland was another call of faith to the international headquarters of a faith based institution, the General Conference of Seventh-day Adventist and its North American Division, with the second largest parochial school system in the world, one of the major development and disaster relief agencies serving the world, over 100 colleges and universities around the world, over 60 hospitals and nursing homes in the United States alone, over 5,000 churches in the United States, and over 6,000 employees in the U.S. Whether you consider the activities and institutions around the world or just within the United States, this is a major national and world body in comparison to any corporate entity, secular or religious. My international experience at the U.S. Department of State was attractive to the world leaders. And my national leadership as United States Commissioner for the Administration of Children, Youth and Families with a multibillion dollar budget was attractive to those with responsibilities for U.S. and North American activities. I served on the world executive committee and as vice president for the North American Division and president of the North American Religious Liberty Association. I was a member of approximately 40 oversight service and ministry committees, chairing nearly 20 of these. I directed the religious liberty and public affairs department for North America, and as such was the chairman of the litigation committee for North America and was a member of the legal affairs committee for the world organization. I was spokesperson before Congress and other interested external and internal institutions. There was much speaking, writing, and many business meetings. Our institutions owned 43 airplanes in the U.S. and I chaired the aviation committee. The instructor pilots on the aviation committee assumed that I was a pilot. One suggested that I might enjoy taking a new plane up for a flight over Lake Michigan. I agreed and we were soon in it with me at the controls. He quickly recognized my lack of familiarity and instructed me in my first piloting experience. I had desires of becoming a pilot in earlier years. Just before leaving the Air Force, I flew from Fairbanks, Alaska, to Fort Wayne, Indiana, on an Air Force jet tanker plane which refueled another plane while we were flying above the clouds. I observed this high-tech procedure right beside the technician who actually hooked the planes to each other with a fuel pipe and fed fuel into the second plane. We were in the rear of our tanker plane lying on our stomachs with the controls in front of our eyes at a window which allowed us to observe the plane behind us as it gently closed the gap between us and maintained our speed to prevent separation and waste of fuel. That was exciting and strengthened my desire to become a pilot. But it has not happened yet.

As chairman of the retirement committee, I was able at times to get some compassion for workers who encountered difficulties in proving their total years of eligible service. There were methods of confirming eligible time which had not been used very much before. And with a special scholarship committee, there were some rules which needed adjusting. These scholarships were for students studying in North America though we urged our students to think globally when thinking of service. One mother called me to report her son, Benjamin, was studying in Manila because this could help him compete for international career opportunities. I agreed with her and secured a written request from a regional conference president, Joseph McCoy. He was reluctant as he did not wish for others to think the rules could be bent for special persons. But when he saw this was not for special persons but special situations to benefit global-minded students and the world community, he accommodated. The scholarship committee agreed with the McCoy letter of request and my support. The world is now a better place to some small extent.

I mention those few areas of service only to give some indication of the variety of my responsibilities. I served in those positions for approximately ten years until I retired. I enjoyed the work, challenges, opportunities to make a difference, and the many outstanding persons with whom I worked in Maryland, around the United States, and the world.

A few months before being invited to serve in government in Washington, I was visiting the office of the president for North America, Dr. Charles Bradford. We have enjoyed excellent relations for many years. I told him that I needed a periodical book that enjoys a very limited circulation. It is the North American Division Working Policy. Most persons who are governed by those policies do not know that the book exists. A very few leaders have access to it. It is not on line and it is not in libraries. He said I could have a copy. He asked his vice president, one of the most influential persons at the world headquarters at that time, to get me a copy. That person stepped out of Dr. Bradford's office for a few minutes and reported back that there were no extra copies. Dr. Bradford, my friend, said, "Give him yours." The vice president stepped out again and returned with a new copy stating, "I located another copy. Mr. Hodges can have this one." That was a small, but not insignificant, exchange between "power" and "more power." Dr. Bradford understood the purpose and use of power. A moving force had encountered an unmovable force and the moving force was stopped in its tracks. I was glad to be a friend of the unmovable force, Dr. Bradford.

We all were surprised, even shocked, years later when that influential vice president retired and I was named as his replacement even though Dr. Bradford had retired some years before. I never sought all the influence he had, I sought to use whatever influence I needed to help persons and to serve where my predecessor did not have time to serve. I could not do all that very well and protect my plate of primary responsibilities at the same time. So I agreed to relinquish some committee assignments which were not important to me while I assumed and expanded some other duties and interests which were not regularly addressed before my arrival. That book of policies given to me by Dr. Bradford proved to be most valuable as I had read it and was very familiar with all areas and policies before I arrived for service. Knowledge is often the difference between power and powerlessness. Prayers are very often answered before we articulate them if we are in the attitude of prayer. My replacing that vice president reminded me of an experience in Indianapolis. When I was assigned there as Special Assistant to the Mayor in 1973, the mayor wanted me to get to know the responsibilities of every city department and the director of each. I spent hours in each area getting to know and getting to be known. I was most impressed with the chief of police and the director of public safety. I quickly learned a lot about police and policing. I deeply appreciated the respect extended to me and the introductions to all the key officers. I had lunch with the director of public safety at a very special restaurant at the top of a high-rise hotel. But what disappointed me was my visit with the director of community services. He knew I had much experience in that area but he appeared as though he had little time to be spared regardless of my clear relationship with the mayor. However, about three months later, a negative report appeared on the front page of the morning newspaper totally embarrassing him. He disappeared from public view and left town shortly thereafter. The mayor immediately formed a new department, the Department of Human Resources which included community services, youth development, office of women's programs, office of human rights, and housing services. I was appointed the director of that department and retained my role as Special Assistant to the Mayor. I regretted the misfortune of the community services director but I learned again that it pays to protect one's reputation, to respect others, even strangers, and not to get elevated in your own estimation. My being asked unexpectedly to replace persons of heavy responsibility and lengthy experience in those two situations was daunting and somewhat similar. I had big shoes to fill and knew I would be watched closely because my leadership style differed from both. It all turned out very well as I was able to build on their quality vision, service, and leadership. The former responsibilities were relevant and helped prepare me for the various challenges in the latter.

CORRUPTION IN HEAVENLY PLACES?

My faith says corruption is still confined to earthly places, even earthly places with professions of heavenly control and righteousness. It is most unfortunate that institutions with such profession often reflect weaknesses greater than those without such claims. It is understood that humankind in all places is weak and need external and heavenly graces in order to move closer toward perfection but some extremes in acts of inhumanity are difficult to comprehend. However, as we accept as true that power corrupts and that absolute power corrupts absolutely, we should not be surprised to find such extremes any place where there is a concentration of power in humanity. Power in humanity should not be concentrated in individual leaders but should be in the people. Leaders should be accountable to the people and to their higher calling.

Faith-based institutions too often destroy their leaders by trusting without confirming or verifying. Senior officials should assist and counsel new appointees in a manner that will contribute to success and help avoid traps of overconfidence and inadequate preparation. High performance should be expected by all at every level. Even at the grassroots level, congregations exercise too little influence in the selection and retention of clergy or pastoral leadership. The cause thus suffers when leaders think they have earned and deserve the honors, recognition, and decision-making authority inappropriately accepted of them. Sometimes those benefits are abandoned by less responsible leaders and there have been times when some have usurped benefits and authority not belonging to them. These acts of wrongness should be resisted in the interest of rightness as they destroy confidence and support for the greater cause. To me, it appears unconscionable that books of working policies which govern actions are often kept from the hands and eyes of those to be governed and those who should share in the governance at the lower levels. How many children must be abused; how many adults must be victimized; how many potential leaders must be mistreated; and how many millions must be misappropriated before a response comes from the "Levites" (Exodus 32:26) and "Phinehases" (Numbers 25:7,8) of our day? There must be a penalty for those without the courage to take a stand for what they know to be right. The last-day reformation is overdue in every sector! During the time of ancient Israel, "No one did anything that someone else should. Whoever would have tried to do another man's work would have suffered the death penalty. Each one attended to his special duty." (Lift Him Up, E.G. White, Review and Herald Publishing, p. 145)

While serving as director of a major city department for the city of Indianapolis, I was asked to serve as full time senior pastor of the Capitol City Church. During that time, I implemented the principles advanced in the book I authored a year or so ago titled, Christ has a Job for You. It is really about human relations in volunteer, faith-based organizations. Those principles worked so well that Capital City was the most productive church in that five-state union of churches and one of the most productive in North America. I mention that because of the challenges in an all volunteer organization and how those challenges are easily handled with much success when operating within certain principles, guidelines and policies. Respect, appreciation, selflessness, fairness, and a full division and sharing of all the work which needs to be done is a good starting point. It is easier said than done but can be done. Remember two words, faith and perseverance. The book, of course gives the necessary details.

I wrote to the leadership at my old workplace in Silver Spring, Maryland about some concerns I have for that institution to become all it can be to the United States and the world. When I compared it to the letters similarly sent when I retired, I saw that I have nearly the same old concerns. My original letters resulted in quality time being given for me to explore in greater detail all my recommendations with the leadership individually and in groups. The recent letters sent by email shocked me with same-day responses of agreement with my assessments and recommendations. My attitude is that we must do what has never been done before if we want results which have never been achieved before. And it is not about money and budgetary restrictions. It is about commitment, courage, compliance, and accountability. There have been great achievements and praise-worthy progress but, whether calling upon the president of the United States, corporate leaders of the world, professionals who can make a difference, or non-profits, progress is not enough. Only our best is good enough and that must be required of every compensated employee and every volunteer.

There is one problem with faith-based organizations that may be worse than with profit-making corporations. That is the lack of unity in the different layers of bureaucracy. An initiative may be announced and launched at the top with very little follow-through at the "boots on the ground" level. I would urge that the requirement of unity be promoted and enforced at each level for maximum results. This also means promoting policies in like manner. Leaders at every level would benefit from such cooperation but they do not know that. Perhaps bigger carrots and bigger sticks would help but I am promoting more education. This education should also show that the grass is not greener on the other side of the street and that if each watered and nurtured his or her product, the other side would copy or follow their lead. Perseverance is a better solution than to lower one's own self esteem by following the followers.

I was invited to serve on the Oakwood College Board of Trustees at about the same time I began my service at the U.S. Department of State and continued that service through my years of service in Lincoln, Nebraska and Silver Spring, Maryland, for more than twenty-three years. I often chaired the Board in the absence of the chairman and was often asked to chair the executive committee between meetings. I was able to give some meaningful assistance to presidents. This was not only true for Oakwood but for other institutions of faith and secular control. These included Union College and Jarvis Christian College. Other services included lectures and teaching at such places as University of Hawaii, Ball State University, Howard University, Loma Linda University, Andrews University, Washington University, Alabama State University, and Michigan State. Many of these institutions had schools of Social Work which received funds from my office, the Administration of Children, Youth, and Families. Not only did they train social workers but conducted some much needed social research. My service on boards, executive committees, and selection committees allowed me to accumulate a broad collection of experiences which could be shared. I was able to contribute to decision-making which would benefit many leaders and others who follow, to enjoy improved compensation packages, more freedom for outside necessities, and appropriate CEO powers. My teaching classes on international affairs and diplomacy at Union College for several years helped many of those students to navigate multinational career systems and prepare for Foreign Service careers in diplomacy. I also enjoyed interacting with social work students and faculties getting ideas for improved connections and services from Washington and helping expand opportunities for careers of interest to students. Some lectures were video-taped for sharing with multiple classes.

On one visit to Oakwood (now University) in Huntsville, Alabama, my wife and I were impressed with some of the new residential housing subdivisions. A builder made an offer; we selected a floor plan and decided on retirement and relocation. I later shared this information with Dr. Baker, and he offered part time or fulltime employment at Oakwood if I were interested in easing into full retirement. I served as director of public relations for Oakwood for about a year and then eased into full retirement. President Benjamin Browne of South Central Conference asked if I would be interested in working two or three days per month as director of religious liberty for that conference of churches, serving the states of Alabama, Florida, Kentucky, Mississippi, and Tennessee. I agreed and continued to serve after he retired, with the new CEO, President Dana Edmund, for a total of approximately seven years before easing into my fulltime retirement again. I must say that it took only a few weeks for us to realize the two or three days per month represented an under-statement or a shrinkage or reality. That was delightful, however, as I got to know some very nice people over each of those five states, and working with great leaders at the South Central Conference offices in Nashville. And periodically, my involvement was expanded to include the Southern Union Public Affairs and Religious Liberty Association which included meetings in the additional states of North Carolina, South Carolina, and Georgia and the associated attorneys of all eight south eastern states, under the leadership of Ms. Amireh Al-Haddad. Some of these were in great vacation cities and others in capitol cities of the various states, in the interest of religious liberty issues.

Of all the benefits in social services and ministry, there is none better than being able to make a contribution to freedom, social and religious freedom. Without such, there would be very few effective services and ministries responding to the needs of suffering humanity. And little would be done by humankind to spread the good news of hope, life with far-reaching meaning, the beginning of all that is good, and the end of all that is bad. Religious liberty protects all that and yet, many who should appreciate that most, give little evidence of appreciating it at all outside their little circles.

Though I have retired from salaried employment, I am pleased to be available for periodic assignments for institutions I love. Oakwood Elementary School and Academy, Oakwood University, Oakwood University Church, and South Central Conference continue to give me opportunities to serve. The several years, volunteer and compensated services, I have rendered have been more than compensated by benefits of association with students, faculty, staff, and administrators. The same has been true of the Bradford, Cleveland, Brooks Institute which allowed me to serve students, youth, and adults on campus and in institutions or congregations in various cities of the U.S., honoring the combined 150 years service and leadership of Dr. Charles E. Bradford, Dr. E. E. Cleveland, and Dr. C.D. Brooks. These distinguished educators, clergymen, and administrators have been listed among my Christian giants of the world for many years. Because they persevered, untold numbers of others have excelled and continue to make a difference for humankind.

When I was first elevated to an executive level position by the president of the United States, it was called to my attention by Bill Johnson, a friend, that my career path, from my early years to where I was then, appeared to have been carefully planned and orchestrated by a wise, powerful mentor. He was not fully aware of the truthfulness of his statement. There was an omniscient and omnipotent Mentor charting and leading as I would allow Him. He wants to do the same for each who will follow Him. Another told me in my early years that I would need to abandon my religion if I wished to reach my maximum potential. He was older than I but young and very successful, known around the world. However, he died within two years in his early forties. While in my twenties, I declined a corporate offer from a Fortune 500 company to the dismay of some friends. Government and social services had no compensation plan which could compete with that offer. In Indianapolis, one of the wealthiest men of the nation who owned several corporations from banking, shipping, and publishing to manufacturing and retail, offered me a CEO position. He was also a political leader, serving in a key elected position. This was to be a new corporation where I would be compensated very well just to carry the title and a public leadership image. His team would be responsible for the product and financial success. General Motors was interested in extending some parts manufacturing contracts. I could not lose but I chose not to be primarily a front-personality with an impressive title, office, and salary. I understood his interest in protecting his investment as all the capital was his. But he could not be sole owner of a minority business enterprise. There comes a time when one must do more than talk about faith. We must show it in denial of self-interests and in service to others. There is a price but the rewards are out of this world - - - in another world, not for a decade but for eternity.

SAVE OUR CHILDREN

The faithful and faith-filled are continually crying out for the saving of their children, while personally falling short of their minimum responsibilities. Parents and families, including extended families have the first responsibilities for children. Earning a living is important but keeping up with the neighbors, supplying expensive toys, and accumulating wealth are not the top priorities. Too many parents are working to make themselves look good as family providers while they are losing their children to worldliness and even hatred of what we call good. They would rather embarrass us than make us proud. The leaders of the nation who are feeding from the government troughs are living high at government expense while refusing to lead our government to help save our nation's children. They close their eyes to the fact that our country has children and we as a nation owe them something.

Parents, families, and faith institutions have a responsibility to educate those government dependents (officials receiving large salaries for themselves and their staffs) on the needs of our children and our grandparents. Clergy and other faith leaders seem to only want friendship and association with highly paid government officials. They should cry aloud and show hypocrites and scoundrels their sins wherever they are seen. If they do not work to save the nation's children, they will be lost themselves from several possible perspectives. They may commit crimes of neglect just as parents and caretakers do. I appreciated the courage shown by Admiral Barry Black, U.S. Navy, retired, and now Chaplain for the United States Senate. During the 2013 shut-down of the U.S. Government, Chaplain Black continued to serve without pay and cried aloud condemning hypocrisy on the part of many persons in Congress who were willing to throw away billions of government dollars in a shut-down but not willing to relieve suffering and hunger on the part of U.S. citizens who had no food and no health care. Clergy persons should display this courage weekly in condemning persons of wealth and influence in their congregations who claim Christianity but ignore the teachings and compassion of Christ. The Bible condemns such clergy as greedy dogs which cannot bark (Isaiah 56:10, 11).

"Action springs not from thought, but from a readiness of responsibility." (Dietrich Bonhoffer)

"When defeat comes, accept it as a signal that your plans are not sound. Rebuild those plans and set sail once more toward your coveted goal." (Napoleon Hill)

"In each of us are places where we have never gone. Only by pressing the limits do you ever find them." (Dr. Joyce Brothers)

Our leaders should be reminded of these messages. Our servants should remind them. If they fail to convey the guidance and wisdom needed, then they have proven themselves to be unworthy servants and should no longer be allowed the honor of serving. Few seem to realize that serving is a greater honor than being served, that humility is more important than greed, and that children deserve more of our attention than meetings we attend just because they are scheduled. More evaluations and improved methods of accountability seem to always be in order. One thing more important is perseverance but it is never necessary to sacrifice one for the other.

Chapter Eight

WHERE IS MY LAWYER?

It is good to have good lawyers as friends and relatives. I have been fortunate to have such as friends and relatives for many years. Sometimes, however too often, I have gone ahead in the interest of time and handled legal matters myself. I have had some excellent results but I will never know how much better the results could have been if I had turned the issues over to one better prepared than I. I decided rather late in life that I should go to law school myself. I was serious and made some preparatory efforts. I discovered the availability of some good law books for a law library and secured the essentials for law school and for practice. The State Department's annual book fair included a complete set of American Jurisprudence, that 60 volume set of large legal encyclopedia books which sell for over $10,000. I secured them and others from other sources for a song, without the dance. Then I discovered that my vision problem would not permit me to do the necessary amount of fine print reading. So, I eventually allowed the dream to perish with the great dreams of many other persons who could have accomplished what they wished had they only persevered. I should have persevered with whatever aids I might have needed for my vision. However, I have no time for real regrets because I do not know exactly where that would have led me for my short term or long term future.

At least twelve years ago, I prepared necessary legal papers to file a class action suit for four billion dollars against the United States criminal justice system. I was prepared to hold a big press conference at the time of filing but I never secured the desired legal leadership. We have seen, before and subsequent to that time, too many persons who have been victims of that system through wrongful prosecution, prosecutorial misconduct, tampering with evidence, misguiding witnesses, withholding and misapplying evidence, failure to investigate all leads, and other acts of unprofessionalism. The State of California Innocence Project has proven over 300 persons from that state innocent of crimes for which they were imprisoned. (www.californiainnocenceproject.org) The nation-wide innocence project has reversed sentences for hundreds based only on DNA. (www.innocenceproject.org) These and other type innocence projects usually only look for cases with long prison sentences. Former Supreme Court justice Sandra Day O'Connor has stated that a poor defendant can expect a poor defense. She confirms that good justice is expensive. Hundreds of thousands are arrested for lesser crimes but charged with greater or more offences for intimidation and plea purposes. Many of these who plea bargain for reduced sentences, probation, work-release etc. are beneath the innocence projects', concerned citizens', and bar associations' radar. Equal justice becomes blind justice when the defendant is wealthy. The courts do not always see the criminality of the rich and greedy who exploit the needy and those who can buy justice at every level of our judicial system. Why do those who can afford to hire large high-priced law firms to handle their cases pay those astronomical fees if they thought the cheap "bargain" counselors could do just as well? Of all the things that can be said about justice, it is not free, it is not always affordable for the poor, and it is not always fair. And race will remain an unfortunate factor as long as African American males comprise less than three percent of the lawyers, prosecutors, judges, and jurors.

What unfair price is paid by those defendants who are found guilty but who did not commit the crimes? If they have limited resources, they are held in jail without bail until they lose any job they may have. If they have limited resources, they will have a public defender or court-appointed lawyer who has a heavy caseload and limited budget for developing a winning defense. The prosecutor will therefore stack as many charges as possible against them to show a large number of years in prison if they lose, making it attractive for a plea agreement with what appears to be a reduced sentence. That agreement then may mean some prison time, loss of employment, breakup of family, loss of property and funds, loss of voting rights, loss of possible future jury selection, exclusion from many possible job opportunities, loss of personhood, and many other immeasurable deprivations. Four billion dollars could soon be exhausted in the search for truth in all the questionable convictions; in payment for all the financial losses, suffering, and pain; including family and community losses. But no winning lawyer wants to accept such a class action case for fear of the required investment of time and resources. There may also be another price he or she may have to pay the criminal justice system. And the law requires that any class action case must be handled by a lawyer licensed to practice in the filing jurisdiction. That is one reason I should be an attorney, to do what others cannot afford to do and to help those for whom too little legal assistance is available. The money would not be the primary issue or purpose. The primary purpose is to expose the wrong or criminality of the justice system which would hopefully help end those wrongs. The U.S. Attorney General has made a start but he needs public pressure to help him do what he wants to do and to go beyond that.

I have had a few successes before the courts and outside of courts. I rear-ended an automobile when I was distracted by a group off to the side. My auto was slightly damaged and the one I hit was totaled. The other driver could have easily claimed neck injury but he did not. His insurance company wanted me to pay for the totaled auto. I refused and defended my position in court. The insurance attorney had no idea of the location of the damaged car. I told the judge if I paid for that damaged auto, I wanted what was left of it from engine to tires and all the other salvageable parts. The judge agreed and ordered us to settle. I told the young attorney the maximum I would pay. He accepted and I paid him on the spot in front of the approving judge. He barely recovered enough from me to cover his lunch.

I checked into a major hotel on a government business trip and settled in for the night. At midnight, I was awakened by the hotel clerk and told that my major credit card declined my charge. I had to leave. I was given a ride to the airport so I stayed there for my early morning flight. I sued the hotel and the credit card company as the credit card company had made a mistake. At our first hearing, the judge said to me, "I do not want to tell you how to practice law but if you do this and this, you will have a winning case." He then gave us a new court date and asked the other attorney if that date allowed him enough time. The attorney agreed to the time and later asked me if I would accept as settlement a gold credit card and a cash settlement of a generous amount. I accepted and called that a win.

I bought a luxury automobile that was a demonstrator or other low mileage car and later discovered a paint defect. The dealer did not correct the item within a reasonable time and I petitioned the court for relief. The court awarded a generous sum as the dealer was not represented. From another dealer, I purchased a new luxury auto during the time when odometers started over at zero at 100,000 miles. When my automobile reached 130,000 miles, the odometer reflected only 30,000 which would have been very low. When cars were traded, certificates were required to state the actual mileage. My dealer who had sold me the first car and accepted it as trade on another new car did not have me sign a mileage certificate and did not ask me any question regarding mileage. He could see that auto had much wear and tear. He wanted to allow me a low trade-in value based on 130,000 miles and he would sell it at a higher value based on 30,000 miles. He was a tad crooked. He then sued me in small claims court for not having volunteered the full mileage information. The small claims judge (probably a political friend of the dealer) ruled in his favor and ordered me to pay thousands to the dealership. I appealed to the county court in the city where I lived and served. I informed the judge that dealer-salesperson knew the mileage laws and should have complied by completing the certificate which I would have signed. Additionally, the representative sent to court was not present during the transaction and could only repeat hearsay. The county court judge overruled the small claims court judge and ruled in my favor. I paid nothing.

I have participated in several prison ministry programs. I became friends with one prisoner who was a diligent prison ministry student. He had fallen in love with one of the lady leaders in the ministry. They were wed but the marriage did not last. The prisoner told me he wanted a divorce and asked if I would take care of that for him. I talked with his wife about it and she agreed to the divorce. I filed the papers and had the wife meet me at court on the assigned date. After we covered all the issues, the judge asked if I were licensed to practice in that court. I informed him

I was not but was only assisting this couple since the inmate could not attend. The judge was not impressed and stated he could have me arrested for practicing law without a license. I could say nothing else but all had been said already. He granted the divorce based on my submission and the wife's agreement for same. I had done my good deed and returned to my government office to serve my country.

During the time of airline skyjackings and before terrorist acts, I drove a friend's automobile from St. Louis to Washington, DC. He was moving there and needed a driver for his second car. My father-in-law told me that I needed protection while driving that long trip alone. He had a small handgun and insisted that I take it. I took it in my brief case but did not think about it again until I was boarding the airplane for my return trip. My luggage had been checked except my briefcase. I informed the airline agent and asked for his guidance. He offered to have the pilot put it in the cockpit. This worked well until we arrived in Cleveland for a change of planes. As I was exiting, two serious looking gentlemen stepped in front of me and asked if I were Mr. Hodges. I answered yes and they identified themselves as FBI agents. I was pulled aside for questioning. I knew the night chief of police in St. Louis was a friend of mine and I hoped they would check with him regarding my character. I do not know who tipped them off regarding my briefcase unless it was the airline captain. Neither do I know what else transpired between Washington and St. Louis or Cleveland and St. Louis. But they eventually smiled and wished me a safe trip home. I had no desire to be a defendant in court and I did not have a lawyer friend in Cleveland.

In another case, I had filed suit against an institution in a county court with all the required documents and all the notarized signatures. I felt good about my thoroughness and my perseverance. However, the judge said I lacked one thing. He required that I have a character witness available to answer questions that he would ask. I could not think of anyone that I knew in that county who would be available at that time of the day. All could be tossed aside until another date which could require very inconvenient travel and other possible hardships. He gave me thirty minutes to come up with the witness. I walked outside, standing on the steps of the court house, doing all I could do which was breathe a prayer of intervention. My name was called, "Mr. Hodges, Mr. Hodges." I looked up and there was a former employee who had worked for me some years before. What a miracle! The judge could not believe it. He thought I had hired a stranger to pretend she knew me. He quizzed her closely and she was brilliant. She humbled the judge with her knowledge of me and my service to mankind. He could only rule in my favor or look small-minded. Miracles surface in homes, hospitals, schools, and even court rooms. The legal profession may be the last to recognize it but some have been forced to acknowledge it. I have only one word for believers: persevere.

A person close to the family called me aside during one of my periodic visits with her at her home. She was concerned and said she did not know what to do with her money. She showed me where she kept too much money in her home, stacked in drawers and cabinets. she had more in savings, checking, and other accounts and investment instruments. This appeared to be an accumulation of savings from her father, her mother, her husband, and her years of self denial. I took her to Home Depot and urged her to get a secure safe for whatever she kept at home but should keep very little at home as a fire or tornado could take it all away in a few minutes. She declined my advice and said she was not spending money on a secure, fireproof, waterproof safe anchored to the floor. She had a gun for protection.

Later she was hospitalized and stated before close relatives that she wanted me to take care of her money. At times, she thought all the close family members wanted her savings. I had told her before that I did not want a dime of her money for anything I had done for her as I had worked all my life and was capable of supporting myself and my family. She seemed to believe that and trusted me with that request. She did not want a Will and did not want to declare beneficiaries for financial instruments. Some people have negative superstitions about Wills. With some discussions with me and some banking officials and one close family member, she finally saw a need to make some changes in her attitude toward these documents and toward her immediate family members. She thought I could provide some protection against some she thought were greedy or may be a bit selfish. She did not want the intervention of a lawyer and wanted me to make her decisions because some family members might have a conflict of interest and thus might not be totally trusted by all others. I had my doubts about everyone trusting me. I would naturally know some better than I did others and be closer to some than to others. How could I make sure that everyone would trust me. Even good people have been known to get funny when it comes to money. Self can rise up when least expected. I needed the wisdom of Solomon and prayed a prayer similar to his.

Finally, I prevailed with a Will, a Power of Attorney, and an accounting of all assets. Death came shortly thereafter. It was my task to sort out everything and make sure about fifteen persons, close family members were satisfied. First, I made sure to all concerned that I did not want anything, not even my expenses incurred for their benefit. I had to do some distant travel which required overnight lodging. It would have been easier if she had allowed transparency so everyone could have had more knowledge beforehand. There were some very complicated relationships and different opinions based on sound judgment, legal precedent, and law. Eventually and miraculously, the trust factor was clear and undisputed. I deeply appreciated and respected each. I was given the green light from each. All were locked into agreement. The law was satisfied and each individual was satisfied. This amounted to a tremendous saving for each and for all. Prayer, perseverance, and fairness worked.

Another legal problem arose while landing in a commercial airline at the Charlotte, NC airport. I was seated in an aisle seat and one gentleman was rushing to get his overhead luggage so he could make his connecting flight. When he opened the overhead luggage door and grabbed his bag, one of those large aluminum travel cases fell on the back of my neck and back as I was reaching under the seat in front of me for my computer case. I reported this to a flight attendant who advised me to stop at customer services for them to make a record and give me some over-the-counter pain medication. This was done and I continued on my connecting flight to Huntsville. There was some pain but it was not severe. However, I kept my appointment the next day and did not seek medical attention until I returned home. There were x-rays, pain medication, and physical therapy. As improvements were made, I called ABC123 Airline and gave a full verbal report, requesting appropriate compensation for medical expenses, pain and suffering, and other inconveniences. The answering agent informed me that when their planes land an announcement is made warning all that bags shift in flight and could fall when the compartment door is opened. He said that warning was sufficient for their liability and

I could expect nothing. As a frequent flyer on that airline for many years, I was not pleased and followed up with a letter to the president.

In my letter, I informed the president that I had travelled the world over on all types of airlines in small and large countries representing the President of the United States, the Secretary of State, the American People, and other institutions and governmental agencies, and had never been so insulted as a victim and customer. I assured him if that was there final answer to my complaint, I would be in touch shortly with the Secretary of the U.S. Department of Transportation, the Administrator of the Federal Aviation Agency, the Assistant Administrator for Safety, the Associate Administrator for Regulation and Certification, the Director of the Bureau for Transportation Statistics, and the former Secretary of Transportation who had recently moved over to the White House. I told him I would be interested in records of accidents and injuries, safety issues that had surfaced in the last five years, pending applications for any changes in services, and other pertinent information relating to customer services and safety. The world would see and governments would react as appropriate for the protection of the flying public.

A few days later, I received a call representing the airline president, informing me that the agent to whom I had spoken earlier was no longer an employee of ABC123 Airlines. He asked me what I thought would be appropriate in order to keep me as a satisfied customer of their airlines. I had some officials in my office and I could not negotiate but I gave him a financial figure double what I thought would be appropriate. He said, "Mr. Hodges, we will triple that and all you have to do is cash the check which I am mailing to you today." I felt like I had just undercut what could have been a much larger settlement. However, I was not interested in squeezing from them that which I did not deserve. I had recently moved into a new house and this check more than covered my medical issues along with the finishing of my basement with nice rooms, an office, and a very nice bathroom for the comforts of any overnight guests.

Some lawyers can negotiate better than others and some non-lawyers can negotiate better than many lawyers in certain areas in which they have some advantageous knowledge and connections. There is some truth in the saying, "If an individual serves as his own lawyer, he has a fool for a client." One must have the judgment to know his strengths and weaknesses weighed against the time that may be involved, and the fees for the professionalism and respect commanded by the selected firm. Good lawyers are also good at knowing when to use and how to select expert witnesses. Some who are not so good think all they need is a good knowledge of the law along with presentation and examination skills. Expert witnesses are very important and require diverse education and professional backgrounds. Our founding fathers recognized that and left open the qualifications for United States Supreme Court justices. I agree with them that the supreme court should be balanced with professionalism, wisdom, and common sense. That allows for quality persons other than lawyers. And if I were President of the United States and had an opportunity to fill a supreme court vacancy, I would search for a high quality person from a profession other than law. We would benefit with at least one such different background.

I have never sued an employer though I have had grounds for suing all but one or maybe two. If one plans to remain at the place of employment, it is best if he or she can request and persuade what is desired. I have had some successes at that ending up usually with a compromise. The State Department was most difficult of my employers. There are snakes and sharks in those employment waters. My most effective tool was good relations with the Secretary of State. Some senior career personnel are enemies of all political appointees. They have problems with the Secretary and any others appointed by the President. With these, you out-smart them and build friendships with others before you need them. Similar problems are encountered in large retail establishments and other agencies such as the U.S. Postal Service. Faith-based organizations can also be as bad as the worse. It is ok to pray with them but you may need to keep one eye open. Some enemies are without integrity. Build your good reputation, be supportive of others, and keep notes of your good deeds and their failures.

I was making an important speech on an Air Force base in Florida when I was interrupted with a note saying I had an urgent phone call from Ambassador Terrance Todman, the highest ranking African American Career Ambassador, at the U.S. Department of State. He is a prince of a gentleman, fearless of the system, and the best of the best in diplomacy. He has served as ambassador to six different countries in various parts of the world. I was hoping he would be honored by being appointed Assistant Secretary for European Affairs. I had visited him in Copenhagen when he was ambassador to Denmark. In his phone call, he was reporting to me that another top career diplomat with one of the honored jobs at the department was out to harm my standing and influence. I had opposed him on issues of affirmative action, recruitment, promotion, and appointments of ambassadors. If he was that upset, he never suggested it to me so I never made it an issue with him. I deeply appreciated the courage of Ambassador Todman to be willing to stand with and for me against a fellow top career ambassador. I was often honored by the confidence Mr. Todman placed in my leadership and his support of my initiatives. But I did not pursue that matter. I always had excellent relations with Civil Service and Foreign Service staff. As I traveled abroad, the diplomatic corps rendered red carpet treatment and prepared me for meetings with the press and foreign leaders. In some executive departments, there is tension between career employees and political appointees but I never encountered such at State. There appeared to be less appreciation between the Civil Service and Foreign Service as younger Foreign Service officers feel they had to go through so much to get appointed that they must be special. Some senior officers may have been a tad sensitive toward me because I submitted recommendations regarding South African personnel matters direct to the Secretary, the White House, and the Senate Foreign Relations Committee and left them out of the loop. They should have been upset with the Secretary because the Secretary accepted my recommendations, made the final decisions, and praised my actions. I worked directly for the Secretary and did not need to clear with others what I gave to him. I respected those times when coordination and cooperation were important to avoid confusion and the sending of mixed signals. The Secretary included others at his timing. Everyone gets excluded at some time and there are those times when those who support wrong, such as discrimination in the U.S. and apartheid in South Africa, should be excluded initially. It was no big deal for me and I did not want to turn the sharks against Ambassador Todman even though he was willing to pay that price and take them on. My next offer from the White House (in the new Bush Administration) was in another agency, career protected and most desirable from my perspective. However, I turned it down as I had already decided on another direction. Secretary Schultz and the new Secretary, James Baker, offered their support for my future interests. I had not been surprised to encounter some resistance to change and some attitudes of discrimination but I was always pleased with my support from Deputy Secretary Whitehead and Secretary Shultz. The regular movement of diplomats within the Department and around other countries helped facilitate the needed change that is more difficult to make in other departments. It was not surprising to see that my actions for change, symbolic and substantive, would meet opposition from some. It was my conviction that victims needed immediate relief more than oppressors needed comfort. The fact that healing is slowly coming is no justification for some to endure pain longer than necessary so others can experience shock-free movement to that which is right. Ambassador Todman and the Thursday Luncheon Group (an organization of minority leaders at the State Department) assured me that I was doing the right thing for the right people and for the United States of America. It was important for America to be on the right side of human rights issues in America, Eastern Europe, the Middle East, South Africa, and every place in the world. And it still is!

By the same token, one must be willing to make sacrifices for friends and supporters, or said supporters may be victimized or put in positions which could limit their future influence. Sacrifices, therefore, may not be sacrifices after all when the total picture is seen and appreciated. But even if there are painful sacrifices for friends, that may justify the friendship. It must not be about self always. It is sometimes about sacrifice for a greater cause than self, as we have all benefited from the selflessness of others. May it be said that we, you and I, are magnanimous. Under those conditions, the battle is not ours. We can be victors without raising a finger.

Chapter Nine

Managing the Unmanageable

Regardless of our best efforts, there are those special times when it appears as though we have located a problem which proves to be unsolvable or under our circumstances proves to be very difficult if not impossible. We can see this often in political situations where bipartisanship refuses to compromise. If there is a desire to compromise on the part of both parties, it can be done. However, if there is a desire on the part of one or both parties to experience failure at the expense of the opposition, the issue is not unmanageable, it is the attitude of one or both that is unmanageable. The opposition may be hated above their love for the government, the people, and the country. Politics may trump patriotism or love of country. When this occurs, the people, a significant number, have made a mistake at the polls.

Let us take a look at some of those situations which have not been resolved after many years of consideration.

When I was national deputy director of the Community Services Administration, I took a look at one of those sad situations. I became director of Community Action after the decision had been made to disband the whole agency. The resources and authority were being redistributed to the states for the appropriate states to solve the problems within their jurisdictions.

I visited the Cheyenne River Reservation in South Dakota. This is the fourth largest Native American nation in the United States. It was the home of Chief Sitting Bull, created in 1889 and is spread over five counties, totaling 4,000 square miles. The population is not that large, totaling approximately 10,000 persons. There are several reservations in the states of North Dakota and South Dakota and all have similar problems: high unemployment and poverty and high suicide rates among young females. Hope is in short supply due to a lack of creativity among public servants and corporate America. What is true there is generally true of the several hundred reservations in the United States from Alaska to Hawaii and from the West Coast to the East Coast. Native American farm land is not very productive as reservations have never been given productive farm land. Their winters in the north are, for the most part, very harsh with blizzards interrupting essential activities, including electricity, transportation, and education.

Housing is inadequate. HUD has built some decent housing according to HUD standards but without regard for Native American standards and lifestyles. The poor and unemployed cannot afford high utility bills and that is what they get during long winters. The HUD housing had no fireplaces so many poor persons built fires inside houses which had no fireplaces. They had central heating systems but few wood or coal burning heaters or stoves. The Missouri River borders the eastern side of the reservation but there are few water systems and sanitary systems designed to utilize this supply of water. The city of Pierre is at the southeast corner of the reservation.

The Native American reservation plan is not working; neither is the education system or health system or economic development system but who cares? Until someone cares in the appropriate state capitals and Washington, D.C. with its ten federal regional offices, these problems will not be solved. The casinos were not designed to solve these problems. The Native American lifestyle does not lend itself generally to community organizing and grassroots politics. They do not finance political campaigns. They cannot attract major manufacturing companies. They do not have the skills needed for expanding industries. They do not have access to the heart strings of philanthropists or major media outlets. NPR is due some credit for helping to enlighten the nation on these issues. However, there are national legislators and other leaders who wish to see NPR's doors closed.

How can these problems be managed and solved? Just as we help solve problems in other countries, especially where there are natural resources that can produce wealth for flowing into developed and developing countries. The United States has sent peace corps teams and NGO representatives into other countries which have made a difference in improving the quality of life where poverty is found in abundance. We have given reservations quasi-nation status so let us give them some of the solutions that have worked in some undeveloped nations. We have provided for the development of jobs in Bangladesh, Vietnam, and other places and we could do the same thing on Indian reservations. Farm land near the Missouri River could be enhanced with irrigation from the mighty Missouri. Shipping by barge down the river could provide cheap transportation for products to flow to major markets in much of the U.S. Training programs for needed labor in low-skill industries could be provided by state employment and training agencies. I was once offered opportunities to found a company which could produce simple automobile parts, such as rubber moldings and tire tools, in inner-cities. We need to create opportunities for persons with low or no skills on all these reservations. They need job-creating infrastructures and life-saving institutions which can save a significant part of our nation. Towel and some clothing manufacturing jobs which have been out-sourced to other countries could be shared with these communities and towns. Wages could be controlled and subsidized as is done in other countries in order to launch significant development. Solar and wind-energy systems could be developed in much of that open space on reservations and sold to cities in neighboring states. Hundreds of health clinics are needed and could be built and staffed by medical schools with para-professionals being trained from the reservation communities. It is time to tax our minds for ideas instead of taxing our incomes for all we earn.

In the world, we have economic isolation, economic cooperation, and economic integration. The isolationists are usually the poorest of the poor and the integrationists are the most prosperous. Within the United States, the economies of the isolated poor whether occupants of tribal lands or ghettoes of large cities must be treated with respect. There must be integrated involvement for these pockets and for our nation to achieve the level of prosperity which is attainable and desired. The same is true for all North America. Mexico must share more in the economies of the United

States and Canada. Economic integration must be the goal for all three, not just limited cooperation among the three. The same is true of Haiti and North Korea and others seeking economic advancement. Leaders must move toward economic integration and away from isolationism and the limited benefits of economic cooperation. The United States and Canada are doing well, however, every nation can benefit considerably from improvement in this direction and in every direction. This does not exclude leaders whom we love to hate or whom we choose to isolate. It is not required that we penalize our economies in order to pressurize the deviants of the world.

We have heard much from all politicians about the creation of jobs. Everyone running for office claims he and she will create more jobs when they have no ideas for such and the office being sought has no relationship to job creation. However, opportunities are crying out for action and creative ideas for creating jobs. New and expanding industries can support millions of new jobs. One big example is recycling in most any industry. Half the things that are thrown away could be recycled. Each industry could invest in such products and jobs. On-the-job training could prepare individuals for such. This training could be subsidized by the governmental entity which would benefit from the payroll and sales taxes received. Household utensils, small appliances, and large appliances are worthy of consideration.

Automobiles are recycled efficiently in many less-developed countries. A quick look at Cuba will open our eyes on this possibility. There has been much talk about the automobile tire. Manufacturers can make this product easier for multiple-use recycling.

The health and medical industry will always need para-professional personnel even with robots taking more jobs annually. On-the-job training for entry-level positions can quickly lead to certain levels of nursing and technicians which will provide sufficient salaries for supporting small families. The same is true for education, daycare, police, firefighting, manufacturing, and construction etc.

The most difficult situation for one to manage is the person staring you in the mirror each morning: self. I have tried to be thoughtful in managing persons under my supervision, knowing that they have the power to make me look effective, efficient, and professional. They have done a good job of that and I have at least one unusual experience which supports my claim to be thoughtful in managing. Jean was an employee at the Department of State reporting to an individual, Mr. R., who reported directly to me. For a month or so, she was on an assignment where she reported directly to me. At the conclusion of that assignment, she resumed reporting to Mr. R. She promptly filed an official complaint requesting that she continue reporting directly to me. She preferred my supervision over others to the extent that she was willing to file suit to get me as her immediate supervisor. I considered that a substantial compliment of my management style. However, there was an old situation which, for at least one person, was not so complimentary of my style. All did end well.

I issued a directive making a change in a procedure in an employment and training program where I was executive director and had been in that position for many months. One departmental director whom I had promoted to that position and thought we had a good understanding on how to work as a team, disagreed in an unacceptable manner. I was the administrator and she had a disagreement with a policy change. I issued a memo spelling out the change and she issued a memo spelling out her disagreement with the change and with the procedure I used for implementation. She questioned my authority and judgment. This she did in open communication channels. Clerical personnel saw her response before I did and the word spread rapidly. I responded with another written communiqué through open channels for all the same clerical employees to see how business and disagreements should not be handled. I suspended her with pay until further notice and personally assumed responsibility for that department. She called with tears in her voice requesting an appointment to see me immediately. I gave her an appointment to see me the next day. She reported humbly stating I was too hard on her and that I had humiliated her before her staff and the whole agency.

There is a Bible text in Matthew 5:25 which may apply which counsels us to agree with an adversary quickly. She would have done well to agree with me quickly which she did too late, the next day. My counsel to employees is to be careful when trying to rebuke your administrator. To the administrator, my counsel is to be careful how you react or ignore insubordination, public and private. And I would suggest that you make sure you have the authority to enforce the decision you make.

Some personnel systems overly protect management while others may overly protect the supervisee. A suspension with pay cannot be totally reversed while a suspension without pay may see a reversal of the pay issue. Personnel issues and conflicts will always be with us. It is important that they be handled in a way that does not hurt staff morale in general, does not appear to be petty, and does not suggest that administration can be ignored. I helped the offender regain the confidence of her staff and made it clear that the issue of concern had been put to rest. She became a strong supporter of my leadership. Disagreements should not become personal and professional relationships should be restored if damaged.

In another situation, I discovered poor performance in the supervision of a person who was to help protect our image. I had made such observations before and had received some complaints. I encountered him as I was leaving work a few minutes late and so was he. I pointed out what I had observed and wanted to know how he planned to prevent these kinds of problems in the future. I thought just letting him know would help him understand the seriousness of the problem which reflected on his supervision, though not his direct performance. He may have been agitated or stressed out and responded unnecessarily negatively. My reaction was firm but I gave him room to recognize the shortcoming of his workers and trainees and to indicate a plan for improvement. However, his attitude of belligerence was unacceptable as it would have a negative influence on his subordinates. He was given the option of resigning or being fired. He chose resignation. Two weeks later, he reported to another organization for a job interview. To his surprise, I was a part of that organization and was a member of the interviewing team. He clearly was uncomfortable. However, I treated him as though we had never met and gave him some easy questions at first to remove any fears that I might prevent his employment. He did well and we agreed to hire him. However, he later messed up again and proved to have some substance abuse problems. I had no regrets about giving him another chance. He deserved it and could have succeeded had he persevered with his issues of self-control.

In a church situation, we had rules regarding service expected by groups and individuals. One outstanding choir was allowed time for travel and service in other places. There was a conflict with an invitation. The director led the choir to believe they were too good and too important to be punished for failing to serve at home as agreed. When they deliberately abandoned one weekend responsibility, a business meeting was scheduled and action taken while they were still out of town to replace them with a new dependable group. When they returned and learned of their replacement and saw that their value as a part of the whole body did not exceed or equal the value of the whole, they were shocked. They could no longer be identified with our church name. They were further shocked to learn that, regardless of their apologies and pleadings, no change could be made until the next business meeting. Again, difficult to manage situations must be acted upon by the appropriate authority without delay. And everyone must realize that no one is more important than the whole body. nity must not be sacrificed for egos or even for outstanding talent. And no leader should claim responsibility for action taken appropriately by the responsible business meeting, board, council, or committee. Standing for the right, perseverance will help save those who wish to be unmanageable, not knowing their needs and true value.

At one international faith-based organization, one very important and talented employee was often used as the face and voice of the organization in special promotional programs and in public appearances. After a reorganization for efficiency, he decided he did not wish to work under the supervision of a younger professional so he disrespected her. He made it known that his public outreach was too important to be placed in jeopardy by ignoring his demands. He was then given the options of working under her supervision, resigning, or being fired for conduct unbecoming a professional and bringing disrepute upon the organization. He was shocked. He apologized and agreed to serve as directed. Again, management or administration must have the courage to stand and never be bullied. An individual with a negative, inflated attitude can destroy the good name of a great organization. Organizational politics and nepotism have proven this over and over in large international faith-based entities. Many leaders are unworthy of the term "faith-based" not because they are dishonest or immoral but because they lack faith and courage to handle people-problems in accordance with law, grace, common sense, and working policies.

At the world headquarters of a significant organization of organizations, one very capable and experienced leader rose to the level where he sought to limit the two primary chief executives and operating officers. His legal reach seemed to exceed his organizational authority. That was somewhat before the time of my arrival where I now had some authority over his travel and compensation. I observed his mode of operation in committees where he sometimes disrespected others, contributed to problems of disunity, and exercised considerable authority, including threats of prosecution, which was beyond his authority and responsibility. It is unfortunate that influential relatives sometimes intervene to protect intimidators. Others complained to me as they had complained to others without results. I reduced his participation in some meetings and processes. I placed limits on his travel and compensation which quickly got his attention. His attitude changed to the satisfaction of all. This brought special respect and credit to me which required nothing of me beyond established policies. Problems can be solved very often just by following personnel policies and procedures. The chief executive and operating officers were delighted that life could be improved without getting their hands dirty. I hasten to add that all the problems and contention were not from one person's plate. Both or perhaps all sides were contributing to the problems which were hurting the organizational unification or amalgamation. Every indiscretion is not a crime or sin but some can have the same negative effect on a body. And while these should not be ignored, they should not be allowed the influence of the proverbial straw which led to the camel's death. One additional issue is that faith-based organizations exercise too little faith and turn too seldom to special prayer for wisdom and success. Standard prayers do not produce the results derived from special prayers. Games of personal competition also detract and subtract from the power of humility and simplicity. Let humility reign.

Where games are played and protocol bypassed with groups as with nations, it is necessary for those who dislike such to play a few games also. In my Maryland work with the NAD and General Conference, I wanted to add pressure on the state of Maryland to stop the execution of those sentenced to death where DNA evidence was possibly available but not sought or used. That appeared simple for me so I proposed such in the appropriate committee. It was soundly defeated by those claiming they did not wish to put their wives and children and the families of others at risk to save a bunch of criminals. I had overestimated their appreciation of justice and their compassion for victims of injustices. I promised to do some more research and bring the issue up again. In spite of innocence projects which have proven that many innocent persons have been found guilty by many juries, there are still those who think if a jury says "guilty" those charged should pay immediately without further consideration. They forget that the most important trial of Planet Earth, 2,000 years ago, the Innocent One was executed by crucifixion. At the next meeting, the chairman could not attend so I was the chair. I did not wish to unfairly use the power of the chair as is often done in different places but I wanted the voice of compassion to prevail over the voices of unreasonable fear. I invited some fellow workers, including the strong voices of Alvin Kibble and Alfred Johnson, to come prepared along with some other non-voting supportive invitees. The invitees could not vote but could speak to the issues. We had the numbers for discussion purposes. When the session was over and the vote taken, the corporate voice urged the governor of Maryland to stop executing individuals until all doubt of guilt or innocence was removed by every forensic tool available. The governor eventually took that action, not because of us alone but because we were a part of a large group supporting human rights protections for all including poor persons with poor defenses. In the name of justice, especially for persons who cannot afford the cost of a good legal defense, perseverance is required.

Old organizations are too often governed by older gentlemen. Vision statements, therefore, get stuck in grey hair. Ongoing change and diversity are overlooked. There is a high price for this defect and for continually feasting from the table of obsolete policies and regulatory verbiage. One manual was being revised and I suggested a change relating to religious liberty in the final stages at a five-year meeting. The chairman of the committee, accepted that as a great idea. Others from North America agreed. The secretary agreed that it was a good idea but that it should have been suggested at a much earlier date according to past practices. This was the authorized body to make all changes and it is not required to go through any other to make any changes. All others may appropriately go through other committees but not this body. The chairman knew that. Others from other parts of the world were convinced by the secretary that procedure which was good for lower levels was more important than "a great idea." The secretary urged the change could be made at the next five year meeting. North America lost the vote. Inflexibility and inappropriate application of practice or tradition won. Another five years may not hurt. However, I retired and thirteen years later, the change still has not been reconsidered or made. It may never be made and a small penalty may be experienced year after year without being fully understood at the policy making level until freedom or lives may be lost and significant financial losses may be suffered needlessly. E.G. White observed, "Worldly policy has a short range of vision. It can see the object nearest at hand but fails to discover those at a distance." (5T, p. 563) That is why we see so much hindsight in the U.S. Congress and so little foresight.

Policy, general practice, and hindsight are important but must be adjusted by current vision to remain relevant. Bullying can also be cloaked under what may be considered tough compassion or other reasonable sounding excuses. Good people may also yield to bullying in order to preserve peace and unity. I saw that when one person officially cleared a requester's purchase of services in advance. The authorized official was not present so his associate, also authorized, gave the approval. Later, the primary authorizing official overruled his associate and would not allow the reimbursement though proper approval had been secured in advance of the expenditure. Questions were raised to a higher authority who agreed that it had been properly approved. But the one who overruled his associate, bullied the authority above himself so that the innocent person who had followed proper procedures, suffered a loss of several thousand dollars. He had moved on and was not there to speak for himself. However, he soon received an unanticipated financial "return" far in excess of his undeserved loss. The official who yielded to the bullying tried to give an excuse to the person making the original request when he next saw him. The bullied official knew his excuse was worthless so the next time he saw the requester, he offered another excuse. And the next time, he offered a third worthless excuse. Bullying takes place in every place, Washington, Silver Spring, small towns, and even in pulpits. Propose a new retirement plan or new work schedule or new compensation plan from the workers' level and you will face bullying. You can recognize it by its smell and sound. All loud persons are not bullies but all bullies tend to be loud.

When I was young and inexperienced, I responded to a bullying situation inappropriately but it worked that time. I was a teenager in the military. One longer term military person, nearly twice my size, ten or more years older but my rank because he had been out of service many years and returned, tried to order me around. He threatened me with violence. He turned to joke with his friends and I gave him a swift kick to his hips. Shocked, he turned to face me and I squared off challenging him to bring his best shot. I was confident. He knew if he won, he would still be a looser for picking on a smaller youth and if he lost, his humiliation would be long lasting. Further, if our unbecoming conduct reached officials, I had witnesses that he had provoked my action. He never spoke to me or made eye contact again. My counsel now is to overcome bullying with a quiet, respectful but firm response. Do not match their selfishness or loudness. Give undeserved praise rather than add heat to the discussion. It is better to say something like, "Thanks for your helpful information or thoughtful consideration." Do not let the opposition see you perspire. Additionally, never acknowledge their credibility and never fear their threats. What really is needed as a permanent solution is the education of management. Once management understands that bullying, harassment, and discrimination are very expensive character defects. The cost of unhappiness in the workplace, needless turnover, and law suits is too prohibitive to allow these defects to be displayed in any workplace. The eyes of management must be opened to these facts. Bullies and discriminators need effective punishment, more than a slap on the wrist or a letter of reprimand. It is more serious than some managers think. Someone must take the initiative and a wise manager will appreciate the awakening. Evaluate the options and protect your humanity and that of others. Your rewards will come and so will the opposition's.

EMPLOYMEN PREPARATION AND JOB CREATION

One special issue which never seems to get too much attention is employment opportunities. This is always true because we never have had 100 percent employment and whatever percentage we may have does not represent 100 percent job satisfaction. Someone is always left with the honorable, though not always desirable, port-a-john service job. A significant part of my career and volunteer service has been in creating jobs, helping individuals find jobs, and helping corporations and organizations expand job opportunities and fairness in the marketplace. I continue to give such assistance and intervene with officials in various capacities. My work and service in the area of Civil Rights have involved all issues with a concentration or focus on equal employment opportunity. As a young social worker in the sixties, I sought to help young healthy welfare recipients acquire marketable skills and employment as a bridge out of poverty. Financial independence and healthy self-worth were the first goals.

My first break in that direction came as I was preparing for my own career in corporate America and I was persuaded to accept a position in a sub-agency, Neighborhood Youth Corps, as its director. Under the umbrella of President Lyndon Johnson's Economic Opportunity Program or anti-poverty program, the Department of Labor launched a major initiative known as the Concentrated Employment Program (CEP). This Neighborhood Youth Corps was a sub-agency under CEP. Other sub-agencies under CEP included New Careers Program, Work Experience Program, Adult Basic Education, Job Development and Placement, Employment Orientation. I had served as management analyst for a city of St. Louis agency, evaluating all such programs in the interest of improvement of services and best management of all resources. I did serve as director of the Neighborhood Youth Corps until I was asked to serve as director of New Careers, after which I was asked to serve as Deputy Director for the whole agency, CEP, until I was asked to serve as Executive Director for the whole Concentrated Employment Program. This was a complex, comprehensive approach providing multiple services to make a potential employee marketable and successful. The names of the component services, New Careers, Neighborhood Youth Corps, Work Experience, Adult Basic Education, Orientation, Job Development and Placement basically describe the services rendered and coordinated for success. Within these components were included special support services for veterans, persons with disabilities, and persons with addiction issues. Trainees in on-the-job training and work experience positions were paid by government funds until they were moved into permanent positions where they were being trained. Training hosts were government agencies or non-profit organizations which included large non-profit health care institutions and insurance companies.

The U.S. Department of Labor evaluated all cities which had been funded to operate Concentrated Employment Programs. There were twenty such cities. They were ranked according to accomplishments, effectiveness, and efficiency. Washington, DC was ranked number one with its number one budget and other resources intended to make it a model. The St. Louis program, our program, was ranked number two for which the whole city was rightfully pleased. However, the regional office of the Department of Labor did not tell us of our achievement. The director there was not totally pleased that we involved the total community in our efforts which included Civil Rights organizations. Those were the days when Civil Rights and government did not cooperate very much at the local and regional levels. However, I also served as President of the Congress of Racial Equality (CORE) and Vice President of St. Louis County NAACP. I involved CORE in a special employment and training initiative where we took over an American Oil Company service station and trained young unemployed males to service automobiles and operate a small business. Each of the Fortune 500 companies could have done something like this. And more, much more, would have been achieved in the interest of the economy, the nation's economy, and the individual plight of the unemployed. On one occasion, I stopped at the station when only a trainee was present running the place. But he was sleep on the job. He should not have been there alone and he should have been awake and alert. I wanted to take drastic action but I believed in "second chances." I could lock the door and send him home or I could give him another chance as I acted on supervision. I chose to counsel him briefly and left. That action on my part contributed to him later becoming a responsible employee on another job, helping others to develop into good employees. Our government gave big banks and other businesses second chances but these same corporations do not believe in second chances. The project did not enjoy the success it could have achieved. The Department of Labor opposed the use of federal funds for the training. Others feared that CORE and its officers, with positive publicity, could benefit too much though only the trainees and community saw benefits. We probably should have built more public support in the preliminary stages especially for the defeat of the Department of Labor's opposition. I testified before Congress years ago on these issues with the Vice President of the United States, H. H. Humphrey, but new congresses do not remember the good of the past and must be informed, re-educated, and reminded.

A larger initiative can do much more than has been done in the creation of jobs in public and private sectors. Profit and not-for-profit employment agencies along with corporate human resource departments should include the following segments:

Develop an area wide comprehensive, coordinated, approach to insure most appropriate preparation and job placement.

Identify and provide services which are required for success in the various paths for individuals needing placement and success.

Train and employ specialized job developers to help specific industries and employers succeed in recruitment and placement of the unemployed.

Involve offices of human resources in all plans, compensation, responsibility, and accountability determinations.

Identification of positions are made with job developers at the lower level of the corporate structure. Thought leaders, human rights leaders, and institutional executives at levels of significant influence should be organized to press major corporate leadership for more. This should include commitments and plans for employment growth and for upper level positions. This creates expanded demands for all goods and services and for the economy as a whole. This is a five-step approach to true job creation. It represents win-win. There are no losers and the national economy wins. The private sector profits, the public sector enjoys an expanded tax base, and the non-profit institutions receive more charitable contributions. Inflation can be kept under control with more incentives for saving and investing instead of over-spending.

The most important factors needed for getting the unemployed into positions are positive attitudes, directions on what needs to be done and how it needs to be done. Employment orientation can help develop good attitudes and can be provided by employing companies, state employment agencies, non profit or profit-making agencies, and even faith-based organizations. Companies can provide on-the-job training or skill training centers can develop programs to satisfy company needs regarding what needs to be done and how it needs to be done. This can be done for a cost to the companies, state or federal government, or the individual if there is a commitment to employ trainees upon completion of training.

This was done with New Careers, CEP, in placing police and corrections trainees, teacher aids, nursing assistants, licensed practical nurses, various types of mechanics, and technician trainees. One unusual example which can be multiplied with commitment was a young single mother who got her GED, became a lab technician at a hospital, was assisted with additional educational assistance until she received her MD degree and became a pediatrician. Efficiency, effectiveness, and a supportive environment produced a pediatrician to help make this a better world. If this could be done in one city one time, it could be repeated in different careers, specialties, and cities possibly multiple thousands of times. The limits are determined by limits on vision and perseverance. Plans for shattering glass ceilings should be created with participation of job developers.

College presidents, other institutional administrators, elected officials, agency CEOs, business leaders religious leaders, and all other professionals should use their influence for solving problems of society beyond their compensated employment. Volunteerism should be included in the position descriptions. Give something back. Stretch your minds, your commitment, and your value to the community which contributes to your economic status. Mayors and governors should spearhead these initiatives with the assistance of appropriate federal cabinet level officials. Political leaders should stop making claims at election time which they cannot deliver between elections. With true unity in community, success can be achieved where only failure may be experienced while working alone. The Department of Labor will gladly assist with ideas, information, personnel, and other resources. Employment and training programs and job creation efforts attract companies with opportunities. Hiring companies are happy to enter a place where there are potential workers ready to go to work.

Even now, governmental agencies can lead corporations to do more though that should not be necessary. That is what "think tanks" are for. There are so many undesirables which could be replaced with successes. Replacement economics can turn every negative aspect of our economy and nation around to the benefit of each citizen, starting with those who always benefit most from economic advancement. Replacement communities can replace decaying communities. The same concept applies to business districts. We have seen much of this happen to many older central business districts throughout the country. Future-centered economics and industries may need a stimulus but the benefits are easily seen. We need futuristic leaders in every aspect of business, politics, and society. And when young minds of children dream of becoming star athletes, encourage them. Beyond that, encourage them to become lawyers, physicians, stock brokers, automobile dealers, property brokers, developers, architects, counselors, and builders for star athletes who would love to hang out with these bright-minded business partners. Just in case they do not become a star athlete or after that career is over, lead them to prepare for a profession which can help star athletes and enjoy their friendship. They can play ball together in their personal recreation and help build a better community, a better America, and a better world together as equal stars doing different things. If we persevere with the positives, we can manage what might have been our unmanageable children, failing schools, decaying cities, bankrupt businesses, and people at war.

All levels of government must place a high emphasis on education. Every child needs the assurance of being able to secure at least two years of education beyond high school even if that includes some work requirement to pay for tuition. If one must work then the opportunity to work should be provided through an office in the state employment service or educational institution. Work and study activities should be linked where needed. One should not be required to go into debt for an education which provides only limited options, opportunities, and dreams.

The value of education to the world, the nation, each state, and each county justifies sufficient taxation and support to make each child a productive adult. And each productive adult owes something to our educational system since each citizen has benefitted and benefits from our educational system. I benefitted personally from what was known as an inferior segregated educational system in North Carolina though I did master the basics better than many who had opportunities superior to mine. Perseverance on the part of committed teachers and administrators and my mother and grandmother made a difference. One high school English teacher, Mrs. Dorothy Hardy, excelled and saw that I excelled in my use of the English language in writing and speech. Special college opportunities and incentives for military personnel and veterans (at Bethany College, Harris Teachers College, and Southern Illinois University) helped me to continue college studies while in the military and upon returning to civilian life as a husband and father. As a working professional with significant responsibilities, I completed all academic requirements for the Bachelor Degree in Public Administration, Alexander Hamilton Institute's advanced Business Management Program, Master of Arts in Urban Studies, Graduate National Urban Fellow, Ph.D. in Political Science, and was awarded a Doctor of Laws degree and more. It has been an honor for me to speak to young persons, elementary, high school, and college students, about the importance of education. It is important that they maximize every opportunity and advantage. The process of being confirmed by the United States Senate two times without opposition, managing multi-billion dollar budgets, and professional service in the White House often have professors asking questions about getting into such opportunities and programs. Educators and other professionals often need encouragement to continue their education and consider new pursuits. They may become students again as they help their students reach for the stars.

It is difficult for adults with family and employment responsibilities to continue their education and dreams of achieving greatness. But they must continue. For those who have not already maximized their responsibilities, hold on and hold off until you get a grip on successes that will help you meet your responsibilities without excessive stress. Remember early marriages and parenthood are the biggest obstacles to success and wealth. Education is essential for high achievement. One should not give up because of unwise youthful decisions. Regroup, recover, and take advantage of every opportunity to gain more relevant education and experiences. However, as important as education is, there are several other very important factors which must not be ignored. These factors are addressed throughout this book and especially in the next chapter, entitled *Keys to Super Success.* There are super stars who do not have a super education. Just imagine what they could have done with more education.

I have personally experienced some of the problems of not being able to do what I most wished to do because of some earlier decisions and priorities. As indicated above, I am one of those that chose an early marriage and early parenthood. My wife and I were married when I was eighteen years of age and our first child was born when I was twenty years of age. I had also voluntarily entered military service where the compensation was very low. These decisions placed some limits on what I could do within certain time periods and what I could do for my four children. Personal sacrifices and establishing wise priorities made it possible to do what was most important with work, education while working, taking advantage of opportunities available, and being faithful to family, faith, and principles of integrity. Some dreams were missed. I never received my pilot's license nor purchased my own plane. It was possible but would have required other sacrifices and other shifts in priorities.

Griggs University of Silver Spring, Maryland, and now sharing the campus of Andrews University, Berrien Springs, MI, has provided tremendous opportunities with home study educational programs for many years. Many others have joined in with creative programs to help the nontraditional students succeed. These are fully accredited institutions with the flexibility many may need. Oakwood University of Alabama has announced an expanded adult program and an international Internet division in order to gain a share of the adult education and off-campus market. Institutions in other countries have developed programs in response to the growing interest of multinational corporations and many governments. The phony institutions without creditable recognition have been largely put out of business. However, if one has questions of quality education creditability, he or she should check with the secretary of state or the department of education of the state within which the office or institution of interest is located and the legality can be confirmed or denied.

All these ideas should be accepted as seeds in the minds of every national and state administration. Leadership from the U.S. President can inspire and reward public officials, administrators in public and private institutions, business leaders, and their own cabinet and sub-cabinet appointees to ensure these concepts work to the extent possible. The departments of labor, commerce, agriculture, education, defense, veterans affairs, energy, health and human services, housing and urban development, and interior have primary responsibilities in these areas and all the others including EEOC, OPM, SBA, and postal service could cooperate in bringing this nation to full employment. Every able-bodied and able-minded adult who wants to work could be working, preparing for work, or caring for someone who cannot work. Fewer dependents would make it possible to properly care for those who are worthy and qualified dependents. Love and full appreciation for country would minimize the need for protection against evildoers. Candidates and current office-holders, get onboard and tax your minds (not our income) for solving people problems and national problems. We must prepare for the future or the future will irrelevantize our children and obsoletize us. Some labor stats suggest that the top ten jobs in demand in 2010 did not exist in 2004. Our children, therefore, must start preparing now for jobs which do not exist. They must prepare for broad generalist thinking while keeping current with technological progress. They must be able to go with the flow which means being able to change jobs every other year. They may not actually, but must have the capability. Today's leaders must enable, require, and motivate individuals, families, children, and communities to do for themselves what they can do for themselves. Tough compassion is in order also.

SPECIAL ADULT EDUCATION OPPORTUNITIES

8 Ways to EARN College Credit Without Taking A College Class

1. ACE <u>CREDIT</u>

   The American Council on Education is a trade association representing all accredited U.S. colleges. Eighteen hundred institutions around the country accept ACE credit; the list includes state universities as well as community colleges.

2. CLEP Exam

The College Board runs the College Level Examination Program. They give 33 separate tests. CLEP credits are accepted at 2900 colleges nationwide.

3. DSST exam

DSST exams, targeted specifically at military personnel, are now commonly taken by civilians as well. They can be administered at military installations as well as local college campuses via the Internet or on paper. DSST offers 38 exams in diverse subject areas.

4. Excelsior College Examination

Excelsior is a public online college located in New York State that's been an innovator in evaluation, assessment, and accreditation for non- traditional learners. The college has developed fifty-one of its own examinations to award course credit in a variety of subjects. These ECEs (Excelsior College Examinations) are accepted in turn for college credit at hundreds of other universities.

5. LearningCounts.org

Learningcounts.org is a new initiative for DIY learners by the nonprofit Council for Adult and Experiential Learning (CAEL). It's a national service for Prior Learning Assessment.

6. UExcel Test

A new program, UExcel offers seven different examinations covering the content of typical low-level college courses.

7. <u>WGU Assessment</u>

At Western Governors University, WGU, you can earn your whole college degree by passing tests. They formed as a private nonprofit in the 1990s, when the governors of nineteen Western states decided to take advantage of the Internet to expand educational access to rural students across the region. Today they have 12,000 online students in all fifty states. WGU offers fully accredited degrees.

8. The University of Wisconsin has a new program which is referred to as, "Flex Programs for Degrees." They are "un-tethered to classrooms" and "experience-centered."

Seven Ways to LEARN College Material for College Credit Without Taking A College Class

Professional certification (eg. Microsoft certification or insurance industry exams)

On-the-job training

Military training

Volunteer work

Travel (especially in a foreign language)

Life experience

Use of open courseware/participating in open learning

There are serious problems with wage disparities in the same workplace. That should be discouraged in corporate America by labor unions, stock holders, boards of directors and executive committees. In education and healthcare, it should be stopped by government agencies paying part of this unfair practice which drives up the cost of services. For the same medical procedures, it has been recently documented as reported on NPR and other major news networks that one may be charged considerably more, obscenely more, at different institutions getting the same services for the same results. It is unconscionable that federal agencies and watchdogs are silent and approve of these criminal acts. When government funds are contributed, hospital administrators and physicians should not be compensated in amounts that have no relationship to the compensation of nurses and technicians. The same is true regarding administrators at educational institutions and other professionals essential for the education of our youth. A reasonable formula should be determined and where it is ignored, government support should be reduced and the savings should be used for the reduction of medical costs and tuition fees. Wherever government funds are used for the greedy, that amount should be recovered to benefit the needy.

The same should be true for elaborate expenditures or investments, waste, fraud, and abuse. The Congressional Budget Office should provide the same oversight for members of Congress regarding extravagance, waste, fraud, and abuse. No one should be too big to fail or too big for jail. In executive and CEO circles in general, they should have the ability, sensitivity, and love of country to limit their compensation packages in order to increase the compensation of the middle and lower paid employees. We should not have to employ labor unions to determine what is right and fair for such executive packages. In theory but only in theory, and yet in theory, there should be an income gap, which cannot be exceeded, between the highest compensated one hundred and the lowest compensated one hundred. In specifics, these numbers could be reduced to more reasonable numbers per specific industries. This need not apply to those who are not salaried and who produce their own wealth of themselves and by themselves without possibly exploiting the time and talents of others. Too often, not only do those on the top floor enjoy a tremendous gap above those on the first floor; some on the top floor enjoy a tremendous gap beyond others on the same floor. All those who produce should share in the production and the profits from that production.

What I am saying is that on every floor of the capitalist skyscraper, there may be oppression and discrimination with the top salaries and bonus prizes being realized by a precious few who will oppress even some on the top floor. The same is true on each side of the railroad tracks, in each racial, gender, ethnic, and social class, some are economically victimized and oppressed. Some whites have been queried, "Why are you poor?" It may be because they live in mobile homes, wear their hair a certain way, or speak with an identifiable accent. They may have excess weight in the wrong places or may have dental defects, wrong family names or addresses. Whatever the social grouping, America and her capitalist system of rewards, with all its good, can often find a way to create poverty, to divide, and conquer. There is such a thing as equal opportunity oppression. But with the proper leadership in Congress, in the Presidency, and in the Supreme Court, we can have a better nation where all of America's children, male and female, Black and white, Jew and Gentile, Protestant, Catholic, Islam, atheist, Buddhist, Native American, foreign born, hyphenated Americans, and all others can enjoy every American benefit to the extent that they are capable and willing to apply themselves and persevere. To the extent that barriers are removed and opportunities extended, with rewards and probabilities made clear, our people will rise to the challenges, grasp the visions, and soar to their most desired goals of service and achievement. It is not all about money. We must stop trying to make money and wealth the standard for others. It does not create happiness or success for all and has made many lives miserable. The recent resignation by John Moffitt as a pro football player with the Denver Broncos is strong evidence of that. He stated he was leaving football because he was not happy. True freedom is needed aspectively as long as it does not unfairly deprive one in order to give to another. The freedom to serve, be appreciated, and achieve happiness is more important.

Where is the evidence that individuals and groups can make that kind of progress and rise to their top? The United States census statistics reveal the following about one group, African Americans, during one period of time, from 1963 to 2013.

According to the Census Bureau's recent statistics covering the period from the Martin Luther King initiatives and the civil rights march of 1968 up to the 50th anniversary of 2013, the median income of blacks has nearly doubled and the poverty rate has declined by 14 percent. Twenty-six percent of blacks had high school diplomas in 1964; 85 percent have achieved such by 2013. And the number of blacks who have completed four years of college has risen from 4 percent to 21 percent.

With employment and training programs of the late sixties and seventies and the work of the Equal Employment Opportunity Commission (EEOC), employment opportunities have improved for significant numbers whom otherwise would have remained poor and unemployed. Affirmative Action has been battered and abused but has made a big difference for majority women, mostly, and also for some minorities. Housing programs have provided opportunities for many to become homeowners and to accumulate some level of net worth. Other programs of anti-poverty and supplemental support for basics such as food, shelter, and health have made this a stronger nation physically and economically. Those who support a strong military should appreciate these facts. Hope has risen and has been rewarded. Now, if we wisely assess and determine the good and beneficial programs, they can be strengthened by eliminating that which has failed. An improved, equalized, and simplified taxation service will provide generously and also allow for a reduction of tax burdens on most.

Governments have done much to stimulate the economy to benefit industries and individuals. When we consider what the Federal Reserve (FED) has done for industries, ($85,000,000,000.00 per month), benefitting primarily the banking industry with a little trickle down, perhaps more could have been done for individuals in the way of extended unemployment compensation. Even bank tellers could have used raises to get some of those families off food stamps. We need a close look at every segment of society and the economy for reasonable adjustments in the interest of the nation. Who has the courage to say or do something and who will persevere? Everybody could. Somebody thought somebody would. But nobody did. I have a secret solution to that problem.

One may encounter difficulties in managing faith-based employees in faith institutions. Such individuals are presumed to be honest and honorable. However, we have seen in recent years that some may be crooks and criminals. So it remains that they should be presumed honest and honorable but should be watched closely as we seek to verify their unselfish and loving tendencies. Their wealth should not be multiplied by ministry, including publishing and speaking ministries. The IRS has a responsibility which should help build trust and respect for the clergy profession. Police agencies should be alert to immoral charges, especially policemen who are part of faith congregations. It takes courage to help keep persons upright and honorable and prevention is easier than the cure. Silent observers may be enablers and should not be considered honorable due to their lack of courage.

The world stage includes war and peace, wealth and prosperity, suffering, joy, fear, and delightful service. Every time a new or renewed conflict starts in the Middle East, there is much discussion about a major interruption in the world caused by the battle of all battles, Armageddon. Even in Congress, there is too much discussion for me to ignore it. So we interrupt thoughts and dreams of achievements and improvements in the world to insert a brief thought of Armageddon. Some may ask rightfully, "What is it?"

From Wikipedia, we discover: *Armagedōn*[3]) will be, according to the Book of Revelation, the site of a battle during the end times, variously interpreted as either a literal or symbolic location. The term is also used in a generic sense to refer to any end of the world scenario.

The word "Armageddon" appears only once in the Greek New Testament, in Revelation 16:16. The word may come from Hebrew *har məgiddô* (רה גמיד‎ו), meaning "Mountain of Megiddo". "Mount" Megiddo is not actually a mountain, but a tell (a hill created by many generations of people living and rebuilding on the same spot)[4] on which ancient forts were built to guard the Via Maris, an ancient trade route linking Egypt with the northern empires of Syria, Anatolia and Mesopotamia. Megiddo was the location of various ancient battles, including one in the 15th century BC and one in 609 BC. Modern Megiddo is a town approximately 25 miles (40 km) west-southwest of the southern tip of the Sea of Galilee in the Kishon River area.[5]

According to one premillennial Christian interpretation, the Messiah will return to earth and defeat the Antichrist (the "beast") and Satan the Devil in the Battle of Armageddon. Then Satan will be put into the "bottomless pit" or abyss for 1,000 years, known as the Millennium. After being released from the abyss, Satan will gather Gog and Magog (peoples of two specific nations) from the four corners of the earth. They will encamp surrounding the "holy ones" and the "beloved city" (this refers to Jerusalem). Fire will come down from God, out of heaven and devour

Gog and Magog after the Millennium. The Devil, death, hell, and those not found written in the Book of Life are then thrown into Gehenna (the lake of fire burning with brimstone).[6]

We thank Wikipedia for shedding a little light on the subject which is fairly consistent with some Bible texts. A broader study may reveal to most that any battle between good and evil will involve bad (negative) people, the ungodly, attacking or persecuting the good (positive) or godly with an attempt to turn them from worshiping God to worshiping Satan. We see Satan in Luke 4:7 trying to bribe Christ into worshiping him. Christ depended on the Word or Bible and Satan is naturally against the Bible and, of course, the Ten Commandments as recorded in Exodus, chapter 20. The first four commandments relate to humankind's relationship (love) to God and the last six relate to humankind's relationship (love) to other human beings. Any battle between good and evil will naturally reveal Satan and negative people trying to destroy the Ten Commandments and those who honor them. Whenever we see such a battle developing, we would be wise to be on the side of those who worship the true Creator-God and honor His Ten Commandments. We may come under attack but we will not need to fight. The battle on the right side and winning side is the Lord's. His people are united in love. Others may be separated by race, culture, or ethnicity. But His followers are united in spite of race, culture, and ethnicity. They do not practice different strokes for different folks. There one stroke is love. That is their badge of honor and integrity. That is their purpose for existence.

When one reads about Armageddon in verse 16 of Revelation 16, it is necessary to go back to verse 14 to see the context and to see the reference to a battle or war. This war is not between two nations or two groups of nations but the kings of the earth and all their followers of the world against God and His followers. It is a battle of God Almighty which would involve the people of God on one side facing "the spirits of devils" and Satan with his followers on the other. It appears from verse 14 that evil is declaring war on good all over the world. Perhaps that has already begun. Those who hate persons whom they may not know and with whom they may have no personal relationship are trying to destroy the good or compassionate persons all over the world. Even in the same countries, the selfish are trying to destroy their fellow compassionate citizens. In the same corporations, haters are trying to destroy those who differ within the same shops. In government, we have leaders working for the same state or country trying to destroy each other. In politics, sometimes we may be surprised to see leaders (the heartless) in one political party trying to destroy others (the compassionate) of the same party. Even in religious groups and families where love is expected, the battle goes on. There is, therefore, some evidence of greed all over the world beginning to battle against compassion even now. Could it be that we are now living in the final chapters of Revelation?

(For more information and your free Discover home Bible study plan, call 1-888-456-7933.)

Is it reasonable for intelligent humans to make poor selections in choosing leaders at local levels or even upper levels of society? Whether reasonable or not, history shows it has been done over and over again. Many persons have been disgraced and even imprisoned after being elected or selected for positions of honor. It appears that lies are sometimes more believable than truth and that many will trust without verifying. Secondly, we are quick to accept what is in print, televised, or even on the internet. And thirdly, it is easy to deceive with that which is visual. Tricks and that which appear to be miraculous are easily accepted. Even if it seems too good to be true, there is a desire to believe it. On another level, human defects in our characters make it easy for us to accept these defects in others. Many admire those who share their weaknesses and they dislike those whose good characters make them look bad. They are quick to justify immorality by saying, "Let him that is without sin cast the first stone." The family, city, country, and the world are made up of people, the very people we encounter with weaknesses, strengths, compassion, and indifference. It is therefore most important for each to strive for that which is good and the heights of excellence if we are to have a better society.

Additionally, for the United States to become secure and prosperous in the eyes of all citizens, with equal employment opportunities and success for all, our highest political priorities must include that which makes every sane citizen proud to be an American. Each should be reasonably pleased with his or her accomplishments, and hopeful for a delightful future. Jobs are key for the employable. All the successful approaches to creating jobs should be continued along with all the creative and new initiatives. Taxing incentives, land acquisition breaks, free trade issues, and other attractions across state and national boundaries should be maximized.

Expanded opportunities for success and a taste of wealth should include:

Maximizing energy sources and resources. Investments in wind and solar are a start. Safe extraction and use of oil and coal should not be ignored anywhere.

Hydraulic Fracturing (fracking) has tremendous potential for natural gas and should be maximized with maximum precautions for the environment. Precaution is very important but should not mean endless delay until every aspect of every issue is perfectly resolved. Advance as best we can will work.

The greatest cost of education is paid when quality education is sacrificed. We need more of the best educators, equipment, and technology to provide the best possible education for our children and youth.

Healthcare protects a healthy workforce. The need for trained healthcare workers will continue to grow as our population is helped to increase in age. Our transportation systems must match our dreams of prosperity and excellence for our nation. Our political system has not kept pace with our needs as a nation. We need national accountability from those who serve the nation and are compensated by the nation. We need standards and evaluations beyond debates, advertising, and voting. Success should be determined by cooperation not by destruction of the opposition. We need more than two political parties. This is required for continued advancement of our nation and our people.

United States Senate Chaplain, Admiral Barry Black, retired Navy, says another source of learning is from our failures.

"We often learn more from our failures than our successes; hence, remembering the Egypt of our missteps can bring us blessings. The Bible predicts that the day will come when sin will not rise a second time (Nahum 1:9). Perhaps this is the case because those who experience sin's failures see transgression with the mask of deception removed. Is there anyone who, looking back at his or her past mistakes, does not wish he or she had done the good and wholesome thing instead of the sinful and unproductive one? Joseph's brothers' memories of failure blessed them in the long run. Having fallen on hard times, they remembered their mistreatment of Joseph and felt that God was punishing them. . . . Remembering this prepared them for reunion with their brother and a life of service and integrity.

"I try to remember my failures by performing an autopsy on my mistakes. I look for the tipping point, attempting to understand where I passed the point of no return. This analysis is helpful in preventing me from making similar mistakes in the future. When the emotions are gone and the heat of the moment is a distant memory, a dispassionate understanding of what went wrong is often more easily obtained. Failure, then, becomes a teacher whose instruction will produce positive dividends for years. These dividends often take the form of victory when I encounter the same temptation again. The knowledge that I am able to overcome something that would have beaten me in the past allows me to celebrate my troubles in victory." (The Blessings of Adversity, Barry C. Black, Tyndale Publishing, 2011, pp 70, 71)

Another significant need for children if this nation is to maximize the benefits of our potential is to ensure the proper care and development of children in foster care, those who have been removed from their homes due to abuse, neglect, or no available parenting plan. Too many of these 500,000 children are placed on a fast track to juvenile justice and then to our criminal justice system. They need a quality education and quality parenting by either their biological parents, other relatives, foster or substitute parents for hire. Older kids may be placed in group homes until age 18, at which time, they are usually on their own. These children and our society as a whole deserve more and better than this. Some parents could benefit from parental training, comprehensive social services, or the equivalence of a "twelve step program." Foster children should receive supportive services until age 21 if necessary. The question from the Congressional Budget Office should not be, how much will that cost but what will it cost if we continue to spend money without results on our current system? It is possible to get better results with the same or less money. The challenge is to tax our minds for solutions instead of just taxing our income. These children and parents need hope, goals, plans, and support for achieving goals of life, dignity, and honor. Perseverance is what everyone needs to exercise along with caution.

We need be careful before we give up what is good for that which is exciting, before we give up the dollar for the bitcoin or bitmoney, or old Protestantism for new Catholicism, or old Catholicism for new Protestantism (bargain grace). Let us prepare our leaders of tomorrow to seek wisdom above change.

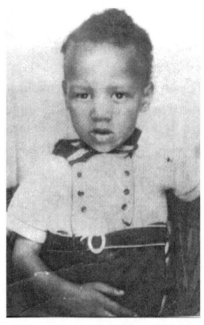

Clarence E. Hodges Standing in
Lincoln Memorial, Washington, DC

Clarence E. Hodges at age 2 and ½

Hodges with Secretary of
State George Shultz

Hodges in U.S. Air Force

Hodges with President Y.
Musevni of Uganda

Hodges with Dr. Samson Kisekka,
Vice President of Uganda

Hodges with Mrs. Hodges

Mrs. Hodges within days of wedding

Mr. O.D McKee,
Founder of McKee Foods
with C.E. Hodges

Hodges and President Reagan

Clarence E. Hodges in Rose
Garden at the White House

Hodges in "door of no-return" on
Goree Island, Senegal, West Africa

Goree Island (former slave shipping post), Senegal, West Africa

Clarence E. Hodges sworn-in as U.S. Commissioner for the Administration of Children, Youth and Families by Richard Schweiker, Secretary, Dept. Of Health and Human Services Mrs. Hodges looks on.

Hodges with wife and daughters (Cathleen and Cassandra)
and Secretary Schweiker

Hodges with Ambassador Margaret Heckler, former Secretary,
Department of Health and Human Services

Hodges with U.S. Senator Dick Lugar

Hodges speaking while Secretary of State Baker is seated

General Colin Powell speaking while Hodges is seated

Hodges and U.S. delegation arriving in Senegal on official U.S. airplane

Hodges eating darian fruit with Indonesian friends

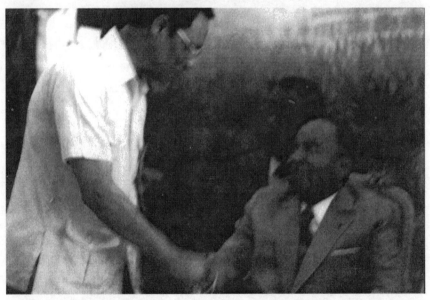

Hodges greeting President of Ivory Coast at summit meeting

Hodges speaking at African Summit meeting in Ivory Coast

Indianapolis Sanitation Dept. Leadership presented awards to
Deputy Mayor DeFabis, center, Hodges to his left, Mayor Lugar
right of DeFabis, with Union President Baxter, right of Mayor

Hodges chairing resource meeting of public officials at St. Louis prison

Hodges rides camel in Jerusalem

Chapter Ten

KEYS TO SUPER SUCCESS

Many persons think of success as it relates primarily to employment and income. If other areas of life are given little attention, this will lead to failure in many important aspects of living and possibly even with employment and income. Health and family life are just two areas which, if ignored, can easily lead to unemployment and poverty. Human relations, integrity, appearance, education, and communication skills represent a few other areas which can severely impact the success of most. One's overall goals as a complex human being determine to what extent numerous aspects of our being and environment may affect our living and achievements. In general, one must have realistic goals based on a willingness to make the necessary preparation and sacrifices. If one's goals do not require preparation and sacrifice, they probably are not worthy of pursuit.

What you dream of achieving and becoming, in general, should be put in writing and reviewed regularly. As you think and review, it may be modified periodically. It may be too ambitious for you to share the details with your friends and relatives who have small dreams, many doubts, and big fears. Be careful. You do not need anyone's negativity. Success starts with your first step. As in the military, it is wise to start on the correct foot. I knew that when I first arrived at basic training as a teenager. That immediately gave me an advantage and a move to the head of the class. To start wrong, may require the loss of valuable time to make the correction. This dream or these dreams which occupy the brightest spot of your mind, where your thoughts take delight in resting, which can give you peace just before you fall asleep and give you energy when you awake, which you find worth saving and sacrificing for, this dream which you are determined to never place in jeopardy because of suggestions of friends or for a moment's gratification; be very careful because this dream as you continue to prepare, by God's grace, is what you will become.

There are five "Ps" which I have found very helpful in assuring real success:

Pray. Praying is not just asking for things or seeking solutions to problems. It is a lifestyle, an attitude, and it is invisible evidence of a possible bright future regardless of the present.

Plan. This is a verb which one must do and a noun which should be written out and reviewed regularly with #1 above.

Prepare. Determine what attributes will help you succeed and acquire those attributes (such as dependability, integrity, selflessness, diligent student and worker, good listener, appreciate opinions of others, etc.). Determine educational requirements for your ambition and meet such.

Prioritize. Put first things first. Take care of that which is most important but never ignore the small issues and the small defects which can sink your ship. Quickly resolve legal problems and family issues which may discredit and suggest poor character traits.

Persevere. Never give up in seeking to overcome obstacles. Never give in to intemperance or to opposition or offers which appear to be good for today but could cost you dearly tomorrow. Never underestimate the value of service in the interest of others; the road to success is very often paved with evidence of selflessness.

These are five steps or keys that will get you to and through the interview if you are seeking employment. For pay raises, promotions, and other aspirations, they can get you to the table or to the ladder. For the big hurdle, be prepared to tell what you have done lately and how you can contribute today. These are good for the workplace, community service, educational pursuits, the achievement of economic security, and most importantly, for family happiness and success. My wife and I have been married for 55 years, therefore, I can claim some knowledge and experience in that area.

I have found that the following will also contribute to success in most areas of interest including your next moves onto and up the career ladder.

Do not leave home without your warm personality and humor. And do not go home without it either.

Show interest and enthusiasm in the specific goal that you may desire in your every situation.

Research and be knowledgeable about relevant relationships from corporate interests to relationships that could lead to community, marital relations and potential in-laws etc.

Identify what you have found to be great interests, connections, and special needs and how you can contribute to satisfying those needs regarding your specific pursuits.

Have notes with you and take notes as you listen and talk in FORMAL settings or interviews.

Distinguish yourself from other possible candidates, when and if applicable.

Make it clear that you would like very much to be a part of that organization, industry or family and that you strongly desire the specific position which is under consideration.

You may find the following paragraph interesting from Tommy Newberry's research.

A 1953 study of Yale University graduates was continued for 20 years with periodic interviews. At the beginning, 3% had written goals and 97% did not. At the end of 20 years, the 3% had greater earnings than the total 97%. Harvard University did a study of business school graduates from the class of 1979. Eighty-four percent of the class had no specific goals. Thirteen percent had goals and plans but they were unwritten. Three percent of the class had written goals with a plan of action. Ten years later, those with mental goals were earning twice as much as those with no goals and the three percent with written goals and plans of action were earning ten times as much as the other ninety-seven percent combined. (See Lesson 3, Success is Not an Accident by Tommy Newberry, Tyndale House Publishers, Inc., Carol Stream, IL.)

I have had opportunities to observe many persons who enjoyed super success. I have seen some come down as fast as they went up. We all know some presidents who have had some negative experiences after their big elections. Lyndon B. Johnson had some human relations problems and some issues of power usage or non-sharing. He, therefore, saw that he could not win a second full term. Richard M. Nixon had some integrity issues and was unable to complete his second term. Gerald Ford's exalted value of his opinions (or his compassion) may have led him to overrule the expressed will of the people which lowered his public approval rating. Two specific acts of George H. W. Bush gave a glimpse into some possible weaknesses which contributed to his failure to win a second term.

President Lyndon Johnson did give us some words of wisdom in his Inaugural Address of January 20, 1965. These words applied to his administration and to our aspirations today. "If we succeed, it will not be because of what we have, but it will be because of what we are; not because of what we own, but rather because of what we believe." It is always timely to examine ourselves, our motives, and our beliefs. If we do not see these as honorable enough to share with others, we should amend and upgrade them appropriately by the grace of God.

It is important to be careful in promoting one's self and detracting from the opposition. Honesty and truthfulness are the best practices. Humble winners stay on top longer and descend slower. The people were not ready for Mr. Nixon to be pardoned. Mr. Ford had a different opinion. Opinions are important and are sometimes destructive. Save your opinions until they are desired or until you are prepared to stand your ground, expend some capital, and deflate every point of opposition in order to persuade others to stand with you.

I and a friend, Samuel Cornelius, were asked to prepare papers proposing candidates for vice president with the first President Bush. We both did. I recommended Senator Dick Lugar because of his agriculture and foreign affairs experience in the Senate and his urban experience as mayor of Indianapolis. Mr. Cornelius recommended Bob Dole because of his military service, long experience in the Senate on the finance committee and his Midwest roots. Mr. Bush selected a vice presidential running mate, Dan Quayle, who had not been prepared by years of experience at that level and the election team failed to prepare him for the heat in the kitchen of politics. Mr. Quayle was more prepared for the vice presidency than he was for the campaign. Mr. Bush seemed to have preferred to win the election based on his long resume of experience without owing his success to an older vice president or he may have wished to give a younger person an opportunity to grow and then be elected to two full terms on his own. Secondly, when he was sworn in as president, some key cabinet officials in the Reagan administration were allowed to go to the inauguration in their chauffeured limousines. However, some were not comfortable by having to return and vacate their offices without that special transportation. They could take a taxi or hitch a ride with a friend back to their old offices and personal automobiles. There are no small things in human relations. And people who slight others eventually experience greater slights.

I have been asked how I was affected by President Reagan's management style. Like Mr. Lugar, he did not micromanage or direct day to day activities. I followed my mission statement and my job description, avoided negative press, got along with my civil service employees, and maintained good relations with the public I was to serve. My civil rights background and my years of service managing programs designed for the poor, disadvantaged, and minorities served me well. I was known and supported by civil rights leaders, the Congressional Black Caucus, and Blacks in the media. My articles which appeared regularly in urban and inner-city newspapers and sometimes in the Congressional Record, as supported by my friends in

Congress, made it clear that I stood for social justice, civil rights, religious freedom, affirmative action, economic opportunity and anti-poverty programs. Therefore, I did not see fit to change any of my positions, after my new appointment, which may have differed from many others in that Administration. They knew what they were getting when they got me so I remained who I was in public speeches and in policy decisions within reason and in good taste. I had testified before Congress on many of these issues without any thought that I may someday work with leaders who may differ a bit with me. There is nothing wrong with differing with co-workers and friends. When two agree on everything, only one is needed and probably only one is thinking. There must always be room for disagreement as I observed during my early years in the Civil Rights movement. CORE, NAACP, SCLC, Urban League, and others did not agree on everything or there would have been no need for more than one group. The Christian in us may individually differ with each other but we cannot impose our Christian beliefs on other Christians or non-Christians.

I have learned some special lessons from many persons. It is great to learn from intellectual giants but there are many other sources, including children and even animals or insects. Solomon suggested we study the ant. Wise persons can learn from such, however, dummies refuse to learn from the wise. There are those who cannot be told anything by anyone. Rather than list all my great leaders of today, I will share some from current and Biblical times and some others who have been worthy role models in some aspects of life.

How we are educated in every aspect of life determines how we respond with our brain cells and genes.

Dr. Martin Luther King, Jr., was one of the great American achievers of super success and yet, he like the great man Moses, only made it to the mountain top. This comparison stops there. There has been only one Moses and he received eternal rewards shortly after his mountain top experience. Back to Dr. King, his achievements have continued for a half century beyond his death and may extend to that length again. What can the ambitious learn from him? Love, faith, humility, patience, and PERSEVERANCE brought him this far.

Drs. E.E. Cleveland, C.E. Bradford, and C.D. Brooks in whose honor the Bradford, Cleveland, Brooks Leadership Center was named on the campus of Oakwood University served and achieved at the highest levels of human service individually and collectively. Their leadership, ministry, and teachings have been felt around the world for more than fifty years, and like Dr. King's influence, will continue for decades to come. They are known as communicators of righteousness who practiced what they preached and teach.

Nelson Mandela, with determination that could never be detoured and a heart that never had room for hatred, overcame every human obstacle. He won the hearts of real humans around the world without trying. His goal was to serve his people and the world became his people.

Sandy Phillips lost her daughter in the Aurora, Colorado, theater shooting massacre. She has since dedicated her life to one major goal: doing all she can to stop gun violence. Though she knows she cannot stop it, she also knows that she can do all she can. Devotion to worthy causes can bring out the best in humanity and lead to super success.

Vivian Hobbs aspired to become a successful surgeon when she graduated from high school in 1972. However an automobile accident going home from her prom left her paralyzed from the neck down. She could never become a surgeon but she did become a successful wife and mother of three while she excelled as a successful attorney in Silver Spring, Maryland. My visiting with her erased all my excuses for mediocrity. She gave new meaning to the word PERSEVERANCE.

Elena Delladonna, a young female professional basketball player is a developing star. She continues to set records being all she can be on the basketball court. But more important to her is the quality time she can spend with her young loving and inspiring sister who just happens to be blind and deaf with other crippling disabilities.

Elena values love of family above applause and wealth. She knows the true meaning of priorities.

Warren Buffett and Bill Gates are heroes and are admired in every part of the world. They are highly successful individuals with qualities of life which make parents and children proud. They are the wealthiest two persons in the United States. Buffett is an investor and a philanthropist and Gates is an investor, programmer, inventor, and philanthropist. Their lives give evidence of belief in a very old principle: "It is more blessed to give than to receive," and they have taught their family members to trust that principle also.

Kimberley Motley is a 38 year old American lawyer, former Ms. Wisconsin beauty queen, living and practicing law as the only foreign litigator in Afghanistan. Her mother is North Korean and her dad is African American. She went to Afghanistan for the U.S. Department of State to train and mentor Afghan lawyers. When she discovered a large number of Westerners imprisoned with poor representation, she got permission from the Minister of Justice and the Supreme Court Chief Justice to launch a practice defending foreigners. She represents Afghan women, without charge, who have been battered, raped, sold into undesired marriages, denied education, and victimized in diverse ways. Attorney Motley is nick-named "911" as she is the one to call when foreigners and females are in trouble. She has been successful in all types of criminal and civil cases 90% of the time. Eight arrest orders have been issued against her without success along with numerous death threats as she drives around town without protection in her SUV. She wears no head scarf. She is respected, feared, and successful. She perseveres!

REMEMBER, those who succeed, persevere and those who persevere:

Plan thoroughly with necessary coordination.

Determine the costs, benefits, and alternatives.

Compare options.

Consider the degrees of difficulty and opposition.

Make decisions based on facts and logic rather than emotions.

Proceed step by step with periodic evaluations and do not change just because of difficulties and opposition. (It does matter from whom the opposition comes.)

When careful evaluation of current circumstances suggest your current directions will not assure your arrival at your desired destination, it is appropriate to make a left, right, or u-turn, as wisdom requires, and PERSEVERE again.

Joseph, Daniel, and Queen Esther served in empires which were ruled by kings who served different gods but these saints so served their God that the world, including their kings, recognized their God as superior. Their faithfulness to God, their consciences, and duty placed them above others as achievers of super success.

"No one can stand upon a lofty height without danger. As the tempest that leaves unharmed the flower of the valley uproots the tree upon the mountaintop, so do fierce temptations that leave untouched the lowly in life assail those who stand in the world's high places of success and honor. But Joseph bore alike the test of adversity and of prosperity. The same fidelity was manifest in the palace of the Pharaohs as in the prisoner's cell." {E.G. White, Education, p. 51.3}

Joseph was a graduate of Adversity University. We should not run, complain, and give up when we encounter adversities. Joseph learned and prospered from the hard experiences of oppression, discrimination, envy, and lies.

One should not be surprised to encounter negatives and adversities in any job. That is one reason for the salary, otherwise, one may accept the position for considerably less compensation. When such is encountered, one should not be discouraged, bitter, or suspicious of motives. At first signs of such, it is best to smile, improve quality and quantity, and enquire if there are suggestions for performance. Document charges with specific notes of events, dates, and witnesses. If complaints are later appropriate, your early positive responses will help substantiate your complaints and your efforts to excel.

We should have learned from Goliath (1 Samuel 17:4,5, 49,50) that no one is too big to fail; and from Zaccahaeus (Luke 19:1-10) that no one is too small to succeed.

From my friend, Dr. Leslie Pollard, President of Oakwood University, I learned that no one is bigger than his dreams or smaller than his fears. Pollard is a tremendous model for youth and young adults and has much wisdom to share. He has experienced super success and is a much sought after inspirational speaker.

Your success will be determined, to a great extent, by how the average citizens of your community and the world will consider your contributions to society at the end of your life. Money, not how much you made nor how much you saved, is your success thermometer. You can own the bank and still be a failure. Your family may have to secure a loan to bury you and you may still be a big success.

"The same mighty truths that were revealed through these men, God desires to reveal through the youth and the children of today. The history of Joseph and Daniel is an illustration of what He will do for those who yield themselves to Him and with the whole heart seek to accomplish His purpose. The greatest want of the world is the want of men--men who will not be bought or sold, men who in their inmost souls are true and honest, men who do not fear to call sin by its right name, men whose conscience is as true to duty as the needle to the pole, men who will stand for the right though the heavens fall." {E.G. White, Education, p. 57}

That is why if I were a candidate for the presidency, I would never sell my influence to the highest bidder or the richest political action committee. Neither would I promise to make life harder for the poor and middle class or easier for the wealthy. My energies would be expended to make life more meaningful, enjoyable, and productive for every American, every American, yes every American.

We need more happiness in the world and in each country. Happiness is more important than the emblems or toys of success. We often ignore the contributing factors of happiness. They include an attitude of gratitude, the ability to persevere with personal pursuits, a desire to serve those who cannot repay you, a spirit of forgiveness toward those who envy or don't understand you, and a positive outlook on life and your future.

I have pointed out a few high profile successes in American and Biblical life. I could have added another very special political leader who has enjoyed many successes while facing many unique challenges and some special opposition. That is our present president, Barack Obama. When he first announced his candidacy, there was no indication of strong support from any perspective and no indication of strong belief that he could secure his party's nomination, not to mention, be elected. And with the strong opposition voiced throughout his first term, the predictors were firm indicating anyone could defeat him in his second campaign. It was said that he had too little experience and he should wait his turn. It was said that he had the wrong name, that he was not a Christian, that he was not a natural United States citizen. And if that was not enough, we were reminded that we had never elected a Black vice president and the country certainly was not ready for a Black president. Some felt he could not raise enough money for a national campaign, and others even predicted that Congress would not cooperate with him. So far, he has proved the political prophets wrong, overall. The whole story must be told by history but he has already done what others have tried and failed without his obstacles.

He has been elected twice with significant margins of victory in both the electoral college and the total votes. He has ended one war which cost us thousands of lives and is about to end the second war which is our longest in history. He did not start either, though he was somewhat supportive of the latter. He has already won the Nobel Peace Prize. And, he turned around our second worst economy during a global recession and has presided over our highest achieving stock market. He has produced a national health care program while working to solve problems created by others who seemed to think the only solutions to national problems were to cut programs designed to enhance the lives of the poor, senior citizens, women, minorities, and the middle class; and cut taxes for the wealthy. Whatever the final chapter of his presidency concludes, we can agree that he has overcome obstacles and opposition through prayer, preparation, planning, prioritizing, and perseverance by the grace of God. There are those who love him and those who hate him. All those who hate him are not Republicans and all those who love him are not Democrats. Additionally, all those who do not support him are not whites and all those who love him are not African Americans. Life is more than race but it does include race and politics is more than political parties but it does include political parties. Therefore, I and all political thinkers must be judged by more than race and party.

Let me point out some successes of a different type. When I was United States Commissioner for the Administration of Children, Youth and Families, one of my many visits to view Head Start programs was to Biloxi, Mississippi. I was always pressing for the enrollment of more children with disabilities who needed the benefits of that program. As I visited one center in Biloxi, I was impressed with the quality of students, faculty, administrators, and facilities. I let them know that I was extremely pleased with one exception. I did not see any students with disabilities. The administrator assured me that they were there though not obvious. She reminded me of my talking with the little girl, Lakisha. I stated I could never forget her. She was smart and had much personality. The administrator informed me that she has disabilities. I leaped to a conclusion, saying that's what I am talking about. If that child has a disability, running and playing with the best, so do I. She said, "Commissioner, she was born without legs. Her mother has three children and all three have artificial legs." What on earth could I say to that? You talk about overcoming obstacles, those children and that mother, and that Head Start center can teach the best of us something. How would my wife and I have coped with those disabilities? And of all the honors I have received, none is more important than having had a Head Start center named in my honor, The Clarence E. Hodges Head Start Center of Chicago. I loved those families served by that great program and those providing the services; and they responded with love. That's the way life is; love begets love. However, questions should be asked without indicating a leap to conclusions. This can lead to opposition and resistance to openness.

Neal C. Wilson served as president of the world church of Adventist from 1979 to 1990. Under his leadership, the membership doubled from 3,000,000 to 6,000,000. He spent many of his early years in African and Asia and traveled the world encouraging leaders and ordinary members to excel in their pursuits to honor God by serving humankind. He expanded the work of Christianity to the Soviet Union and Eastern Europe, building churches, administrative buildings, and publishing houses in that land which did not know religious freedom. He gave attention to Africa, India, Asia, South America, and Inter America that had never been seen before. In 1981 in Takoma Park, Maryland, I dropped in on a meeting of 300 leaders from around the world with hundreds of others just observing like me. We had met briefly while I lived in Indianapolis but had not seen each other for several years.

As I entered the auditorium, before I could find a seat, this world class leader interrupted this meeting which he was chairing and announced that I had just entered. He proceeded to report that I had recently been appointed by the President of the United States and confirmed by the United States Senate to serve as Commissioner of Children and Families with a multibillion dollar budget overseeing and protecting the children and families of this great country. He asked for a warm welcome and asked that I come to the microphone and say a word of greetings to these leaders from around the world. He knew at that time, if he ever had a reasonable need for my services, he could count on me.

We talked periodically after that. He sent me a very special edition of the book, The Desire of Ages, as a token of our friendship. While I was at the State Department, after a long flight from Washington, D.C. to Singapore, I wanted only a shower and a good night's sleep in preparation for diplomatic appointments in a few hours as it was 2:30 a.m. But the phone rang as I entered my hotel room. The caller was Neal C. Wilson. The CIA would have had trouble locating me but not Elder Wilson. He wanted me to intercede for him to visit and meet with Japanese leaders. He wanted to secure permission for Medical School graduates to be able to take required exams on a day other than Saturday for the practice of medicine. I was able to get the U.S. Ambassador, Mike Mansfield, to support Elder Wilson on this human rights issue. Arrangements were made for the two to meet in Tokyo. Ambassador Mansfield then arranged for them to meet with appropriate Japanese leadership. All obstacles were removed for all medical students as Elder Wilson wished. He was a smooth diplomat himself and a fine Christian international gentleman. He was a master of preparing for challenges, building relationships, and persevering. In 1988, what happened in Takoma Park, Maryland, was repeated in

Nairobi, Kenya, and again somewhat in Minneapolis, Minnesota, where he presented to me a beautiful bronze torch. That friendship with Elder Wilson has continued with his son, Dr. Ted, who has also ascended to the presidency with his father's skills and commitment to righteous principles. I informed Elder Wilson I would be spending some days in Lusaka, Zambia, when I left Kenya and I needed to know where I could worship there. He gave me an address. My American Embassy chauffer had no trouble finding it so I arrived timely and took a seat in the rear. Suddenly, I was approached and asked my name. I responded and was promptly informed that I was the guest speaker for the day in this large, lovely, filled church. This was a tremendous experience that I shall never forget. I attended a wedding the next day which lasted seven hours and I enjoyed this beautiful educational ceremony.

There were three mayors of times past who were very strong. I mention these because we no longer have such city government systems which allow for strong mayors. They had the ability and authority to make decisions on the spot without consulting others and they could make things happen to the liking of the citizens. Mayor Richard Daly was one such official in Chicago. A reporter questioned him once about nepotism and asked why he gave an insurance contract to his son. The mayor asked, "When did it become wrong for a father to help his son? This is America where we believe in the family. We need stronger families to save our children." Another example was Mayor Richard Lee of New Haven, Connecticut. I periodically visited with him as ex-mayor when I was at Yale University in the seventies. He shared with me a situation when he was first elected mayor. The police chief was non-political, had served many years with several mayors and ran the department as he chose. He was very popular. He entered the mayor's office and slammed his auto and office keys on the mayor's desk, stating he was prepared to remain as chief only under the continued conditions of his service for the past several years. The mayor scooped up the keys and informed the chief that there was a new mayor and that this mayor would run the city, not the police chief. He thanked the chief for his years of service and told him to close the door on his way out. He made the chief beg for his job and his keys and never had a conflict with him over power again. I enjoyed many stories of using power to serve the people and keeping in line those who would like to abuse it.

The third mayor with the first name of Richard was Richard Lugar of Indianapolis. My earlier civil rights experience often involved mayors and police chiefs. I had repeatedly seen the police chief of St. Louis show his independent power with the mayor when policemen abused power in racial situations and the chief would not let the mayor take corrective action. This was true in many cities where the chief and policemen were untouchables. It was not that way in Indianapolis. The morning newspaper carried a front page story of corruption in the police department with pictures showing strange connections between policemen and crooks. The mayor called a press conference for early afternoon that same day and informed the public that he had asked for and received the resignation of Chief Winston Churchill due to his now lack of confidence in the chief's leadership for the Indianapolis Police Department. The mayor then announced that he had selected a new chief from outside the department, a college professor in law enforcement. He also appointed two new deputy chiefs replacing the former deputy chief. There was no blue ribbon commission to search and recommend. The mayor spoke and it was done and the department fell in line as he started a process of cleaning up and cleaning out those who had violated the trust and honor extended to them.

When leaders are afraid to lead, followers fail to follow and the people suffer. High moral standards are required of leaders and public servants. Traps are set. Avoid them. I flew into Manila a few days before Christmas to look at some diplomatic and security issues. After my necessary reading on the long flight, I thought I would get a nap but two ladies sitting with me were too friendly for that. One was a nun and the other a frequent traveler to the United States and other parts of the world. Travelers are always interested in relationships which can remove delays from their travel visas. Unless they had something special to offer our embassy and our national interest, I had nothing to offer them but a friendly conversation. I was invited to the young lady's home to have dinner with her family. Her husband was a university professor with information and influence and they prepared a nice vegetarian meal to introduce a foreigner to Christmas in the Philippines. In one of my meetings at the embassy, I was impressed with my power when I pounded the table to make a point and the whole room shook. I tried it again and was told it was just a small earth quake. My humility returned. I did introduce my new Filipino friends to an

American contact just in case there could be some American benefit with the educational community. All went well and I returned to Washington after brief visits to Singapore and Hong Kong.

Some months later, to my surprise, the attractive, young, professional lady from Manila showed up at the State Department in Washington. I suspected there was a special request but there was not, just a friendly visit, until it was time for her to go. She had a free evening. "Perhaps dinner and some special time together, she suggested." I could see clearly. This was the same old trap set for Joseph. This may have been for personal reasons or it could have been a national political ploy. I've seen it many times in different settings with different bait but it was the same old trap. It continues to destroy families, careers, and futures. Many have traded their entire futures for a few hours, a few days, or possibly more but too late, they learn they received too little for all they lost. When you see it coming, don't enjoy the flattery of a moment, testing to see how much rope is available for your hanging. Never toy with another's mind or one day you will discover that it was your mind being misused.

To achieve note-worthy success: PERSEVERE!

Set goals with written plans: Educational, Social, Physical, Professional, Economic/Financial (1 year, 5 years, 10 years)

Daily: Observe reading or listening inspirational time, and remember physical exercise. Organize your to-do list, keep appointments and meet deadlines, mentally refresh goals and plans. Protect your health and energy with breakfast like a king, lunch like a professional golfer, and dinner like an airline pilot. If you do not know any of these, try heavy, medium, and light. Get sufficient rest, water, and practice temperance.

Regularly, expand your network, collect business cards and e-mail addresses, manage your Internet time, be an active member of two or more clubs such as religious, professional, social (Rotary, Economic, athletic, etc,). Guard against over-committing. Establish a reputation for serving well. Help someone who cannot do anything for you and assist someone who can assist you.

Be careful to perfect your writing and speaking skills. Watch your opinions; do not share too many especially on politics, religion, sports, and your accomplishments. Be sensitive to the sensitivities of others, particularly to groups in which you are not a part. Observe principles of integrity. Your reputation deserves protection. Read. Be informed. Be humble.

As we near the end of this publication, it should be clear that, though perseverance is the chief topic, faith is prominent. I have discovered a prominence of faith around the world, even among non-believers. There have been some recent discoveries regarding our universe. According to a report on National Public Radio on November 6, 2013: "A team of planet hunters estimates that about 22 percent of the sun-like stars in our galaxy may have planets about the size of Earth that are bathed in similar amounts of sunlight — and potentially habitable. That's the conclusion of a new analysis of observations taken by NASA's Kepler Space Telescope, which was launched in 2009 to hunt for potentially habitable Earth-like planets around other stars."

Some of these scientific analysts have concluded that there are some 20 to 40 billion earth-like planets with lukewarm temperatures in the Milky Way. So reported NPR news (Nell Greenfieldboyce), November 5, 2013. Whatever these scientists believe to be the source of these planets and the probable numbers of others requires some faith. The other 200 billion galaxies in our universe could each have billions of Earth-like planets. With a reasonable percentage possibly being inhabited like Planet Earth, faith in something is reasonable. Their faith must reach beyond the Kepler Space Telescope. Therefore the faith referenced herein applies to that which is religion-based and also that which is elsewhere-based. For the "big bang" theorists, there must have been a lot of big banging going on. Faith is a ladder which enables humankind to think, dream, and reach beyond self and Planet Earth, and the telescopes launched from Planet Earth. May we continue to persevere in faith.

At an early age, I made some serious commitments to the God I serve. One relates to my worship time with Him. In the military, a chaplain assured me that he would take care of that with a note from him which I should keep always. It worked in my early training but months later, it did not work in a new military installation. I was given a work schedule which took me two hours over my early commitment. I chose to honor the Bible Sabbath of Exodus 20:8-11 in accordance with Jewish, Seventh-day Baptist, Seventh-day Christians, and Seventh-day Adventist teachings. I explained and was told that I had to convince another officer, a first lieutenant. I met with the lieutenant and he told me that I had to get my priorities straight or everyone would want to play that game. God's requirements were adjusted to comply with the military's. I told him the Air Force did not out rank God with me and that for the 12 hour shift, I was willing to work 10 hours and for someone else to cover two hours for me, I would work another 12 hours for them. That should have been evidence of my serious commitment without the thought of a game. He said no. You will follow the schedule or you will pay a tremendous price with the loss of your freedom, embarrassing pain to your parents, the problem of joblessness when you're kicked out of the military and he ranted on with threats, pounding the desk for what appeared to be a very long time. Each time he paused, I said, regardless of the consequences, I can only do what I said I would do. He condemned my religious beliefs. He condemned me for having been brainwashed into being so different from mainstream denominations. He challenged me to prove a Bible basis for my beliefs. I decided to follow the practices of Christ as stated in Luke 4:16 and Paul in Acts 13:42-44. He tried the equivalent of religious persecution, "weatherboarding." He had promised that he could break the will of this young teenager from the back roads of North Carolina. He would try additional psychological warfare approaches and press with more threats until the door flew open without a knock. The lieutenant's boss, a major, stepped in stating, "I have heard enough. This young airman is serious. We need more with commitments of moral integrity, not fewer." He then said to me, "As long as I am in the Air Force, you will have your religious freedom and will not be put through anything like this again." I was tested and passed the test. There were more tests through the years but I did not have to take that one again. The lieutenant was speechless with his chin almost touching the desk. I share this experience for the benefit of anyone who makes a commitment to his God. Life, liberty, and the pursuit of happiness are a part of America.

When I moved from St. Louis to Indianapolis, I became friends with Lawrence Shepherd whom I had met in St. Louis. He was pastoring a special church in Indianapolis, Capitol City. He shared with me some of their special projects, one of which raised funds in the community to assist persons in need, educational programs, and victims of natural disasters. These funds were pooled to benefit persons in need any place in the world. However, the city of Indianapolis allowed them to solicit funds only in November of each year. He said they needed permission to raise funds especially in December when they could promote the Christmas spirit with the singing of carols and other beautiful music. I raised the issue to the mayor and urged approval for permits to include December and other appropriate times for such an outstanding project known as "Ingathering." The mayor agreed and stated that Pastor Shepherd should be on the Charity Solicitation Commission where approval is granted or denied. I saw this as another issue of religious freedom and followed through on all the procedures until Pastor Shepherd was appointed by the mayor and sworn in as a commissioner. Capitol City then began receiving their annual permits for the entire year to solicit funds whenever, however, and wherever they chose. All Americans should support all the freedoms of the Bill of Rights with words, actions, and financial sacrifice.

President Lyndon Johnson stated on January 20, 1965, as recorded in his presidential papers, "Justice requires us to remember that when any citizen denies his fellow, saying 'His color is not mine,' or 'His beliefs are strange and different,' in that moment he betrays America. Liberty was the second article of our covenant. It was self government. It was our Bill of Rights. But it was more. America would be a place where each man could be proud to be himself: stretching his talents, rejoicing in his work, important in the life of his neighbors and his nation."

President John F. Kennedy is widely quoted as having said, "Let every nation know, whether it wishes us well or ill, that we shall pay any price, bear any burden, meet any hardship, support any friend, oppose any foe, in order to assure the survival and the success of liberty. This much we pledge and more." (See J.F.K. Presidential Papers, January 20, 1961.)

I have mentioned many factors of success beyond social and economic status and hope the youth of today will embrace many of these aspects of success when they replace our current generation. I want to go back to two earlier names mentioned in this chapter, Bill Gates and Warren Buffett. They are largely known for their wealth and financial genius. However, they are greater persons because of their generosity, their philanthropy, their compassion for humanity. And I hope the reading of this book may inspire some to see the importance of giving back to the world which has done so much for the successful. History shows that the super successful who are admired most by the world are liberal in their sharing. That attitude is not acquired after the acquisition of wealth. Children may learn to share their nickels and dimes. Some successful individuals are liberal with religious causes, some with suffering humanity, others with important secular institutions, and still others with many great causes. Some persons with very little give fifteen percent of their income to faith causes and another five percent to mixed charities. They have shown that one does not need wealth to share fifteen, twenty, or thirty percent of their income with worthy faith and humanitarian causes. It only takes commitment and planning. Families with several young children and those with children in private schools understand this issue of planning and prioritizing. You will be honored and rewarded if you pursue such commitment and planning. As you persevere, you will achieve, in your sphere, super success.

The following is quoted from the second paragraph of the United States Declaration of Independence:

"We hold these truths to be self-evident, that all men are created equal, that they are endowed by their Creator with certain unalienable Rights, that among these are Life, Liberty and the pursuit of Happiness.--That to secure these rights, Governments are instituted among Men, deriving their just powers from the consent of the governed, --That whenever any Form of Government becomes destructive of these ends, it is the Right of the People to alter or to abolish it, and to institute new Government, laying its foundation on such principles and organizing its powers in such form, as to them shall seem most likely to effect their Safety and Happiness." (See the Appendix at the end of this book and Article 18 of the United Nations Proclamation on Human Rights also in the Appendix).

The full documents (The Declaration of Independence and the Bill of Rights) are included in this book. Periodically, it is necessary to remind some employers that this is America where liberty trumps work schedules. The United States Equal Employment Opportunity Commission (EEOC) enforces laws of freedom in the workplace. See that Web site (www.eeoc.gov) for specifics in this regard. The First Amendment to the United States Constitution also addresses the issue of religious freedom. Any true American should clearly understand that religious liberty enjoys strong support in the United States of America and each American should stand up for same.

I learned as a teenager that anyone with a vision, a goal or simply a thought for the future, that the first step toward failure, is to forget, ignore, or deny from where or from whom you came. The youth and adult heroes of Biblical history and the early history of this nation never forgot their past and the principles of their parents and communities. And when we climb above the socio-economic and educational levels of our past, we must continually reach back and contribute to the betterment of those whom we think are somewhat behind. That especially applies to our parents and siblings. And the community at large also, must never be forgotten by those to whom they gave a social, educational, economic, or a psychological boost.

In several places I have stressed the need for persevering and prioritizing. One excellent example of this importance is represented in the name: Steve Jobs, the founder of the Apple Computer Company. On one occasion, his physician reportedly advised him in very serious tones, to get his priorities in order because his life expectancy was not very long. That advice was considered most important to Jobs. He always believed in prioritizing but this required some plans that would remain in place beyond his life. Jobs died with six months of college education and seven billion dollars. His love of family and preparation for his last days gave him the peace that all other accomplishments could not equal. To those who would consider my words, I say, think, plan, prioritize, and persevere.

The issue of success should be given careful thought from a comprehensive perspective. One may be a failure and consider himself a success. Some view the achievement of wealth as success even though the family has disintegrated and the mental state of each is miserable. It may then be realized that the goal of wealth set and achieved was a failure in itself. It may then be too late to make the necessary adjustments to reverse the negative impact on all those adversely affected, from family to friends to co-workers, to community to those which could have been helped, to sufferers which could have been healed, to one's self which could have been saved from whatever may later be feared most. The achievement of goals by including harmful relationships or a compromise of integrity, or trampling on the golden rule or by denying the god of your conscience is tantamount to the achievement of a goal laced with a social, economic, or psychological deadly poison. So, don't go there.

For those who have accepted the guiding principles of any particular religion should seek to be faithful to those principles. Faith and worship are important aspects of success. When we consider that God has created 200 billion galaxies in this universe, we should have no doubts about His ability to perform miracles and answer prayers. And when we consider the love and sacrifice expressed in John 3:16, we should have no doubts about His willingness to hear and answer our prayers. As we believe, we should seek and determine what is most reasonable for us to pursue and expect. We can also learn from others and then share as we learn and advance.

My approach, which I suggest for consideration, is a series of goals requiring a series of small steps which will insure big achievements before the end. In reverse order with the end being first, it could be one's last breath being one of peace, love, and happiness and before that, a retirement with comfort and the ability to contribute to the betterment of others, and before that, a career respected by friends and family, and before that, opportunities to serve and sacrifice and make a visible difference within my possible range of influence, and before that preparation for service and building including the most appropriate education, and before that, commit to a lifestyle which will protect one's mental, physical, spiritual, and economic well-being. There are many goals, plans or baby steps and major events (degrees, marriage, houses, cars, children, hobbies, travels, career upgrades, etc.) which can be inserted as circumstances develop. If one is serious about goals and plans, they should be reduced to writing and reviewed for adjustments periodically. For me, my very last step will be to rejoice for the grace of eternal life extended by my God and Savior. And since I will never know the timing of that very last step, I must be prepared for that to be inserted at any point along the way. If I can help others make such preparations and important steps, my comprehensive success will be multiplied with joy beyond anticipation. For all the good that I have received, whether mentioned herein or not, I owe the world an attitude of gratitude.

Mary Barra, 52 years of age, joined the General Motors Corporation work force thirty-three years ago as a co-op student or intern. She is remembered as an engineering student with people skills stronger than her engineering potential. She completed her engineering studies and added an MBA degree to her resume. She persevered in a man's world of top management at GM earning $4.85 million in 2012 and was selected in 2013 to be the new Chief Executive Officer (CEO) for GM.

From that accomplishment, and with Janet Yellen now in place as chair of the Federal Reserve Board, it is clear in America that all the glass ceilings have been shattered. Perhaps not destroyed but shattered. Young Americans and youth of the world can say, "What has always been will not always be. Santa may not always be male and the day is coming when none will be second to none."

I am particularly honored to have been identified with Dr. King in my successes with the freedom and fairness for sanitation workers in Indianapolis; with Mrs. King and my international achievements in my service on the M.L. King Holiday Commission; with Nelson Mandela in my push at the State Department and in South Africa for South Africans' freedom and justice; and for my success with many others helping to protect and add funding for Head Start against strong opposition.

Thanks for your consideration of my thoughts and recommendations, especially if you are a candidate for the U.S. presidency. Much success to you; and may your achievements and contributions soar far beyond mine. Persevere!

APPENDIX

This section includes some very important information which should be helpful for every citizen of the United States and particularly those who wish to serve this country in an honorable position, to be compensated by the people of the United States as public servants of said people. It is hoped that said public servants and leaders in government, community, educational, and faith-based institutions will never forget they are the servants and the people are the employers. They should serve with an attitude of gratitude and should never feel that they deserve more than the people deserve in the way of special privileges or even compensation beyond the range of the average citizen. This very important information referred to above is included in the following documents:

Some Areas of Civic Service (past and or present) by Clarence E. Hodges

The Bill of Rights (First Ten Amendments to the U.S. Constitution)

The United States Declaration of Independence

The United Nations Universal Declaration of Human Rights

Civic Service and Community Leadership
Clarence E. Hodges
Servant Leader

CIVIC SERVICE (a few areas of past and or present service by C.E. Hodges):

Vice Chairman, Board of Trustees, Oakwood University, Huntsville, AL

Member, Board of Trustees, Union College, Lincoln, NE

Member, Board of Trustees, Jarvis Christian College, Hawkins, Texas

Member, Board of Trustees, Hadley Community Hospital, Washington, DC

Member, Board of Directors, Project Patch, Portland, OR

Chairman, International Affairs Committee, Martin Luther King Holiday Commission

President, St. Louis Metropolitan Congress of Racial Equality (CORE)

Vice President, St. Louis County NAACP

Life Member, NAACP

Member, Indianapolis Economic Forum

President and Chairman, Youth Development Foundation

Chairman of the Board, Indianapolis Community Action Against Poverty, Inc.

Member, Board of Directors, Indianapolis Big Brothers

Chairman, Human Rights Commission, City of Lincoln, NE

Chairman, Nebraska Governor's Task Force on Urban Development

Chairman, Lincoln 2000 Committee for Graduation

Chairman, Indianapolis Urban League, Task Force on School Violence

Member, Executive Committee, General Conference of Seventh-day
   Adventists
President, North American Religious Liberty Association
Member, Board of Directors, TEACH International
Chairman, Board of Directors, Pan African Development Corp.
Member, Amnesty International
Member, Southern Poverty Law Center
Visiting Professor, George Warren Brown School of Social Work,
   Washington University, St. Louis, MO
Visiting Professor, School of Social Work, University of Hawaii
Visiting Professor, Columbia Union College, Takoma Park, MD
Visiting Professor, Oakwood University, Huntsville, AL
Visiting Professor, Ball State University, Indianapolis, IN
Adjunct Professor, Union College, Lincoln, NE
Candidate for U.S. Congress, 1980, 11th District, Indiana
Numerous articles: U.S. Congressional Record, Message Magazine,
   Adventist Review, Review and Herald Leadership, St. Louis Argus,
   St. Louis American, Indianapolis Recorder

LISTINGS AND SPECIAL HONORS:

Schools/educational centers named in honor of C.E. Hodges in
   Chicago, IL and in Ghana, West Africa
Scores of awards including honorary doctorates, keys to several cities,
   honorary citizenship certificates from several cities and states, and
   listings in:
Who's Who In America
Who's Who In American Politics
Who's Who In Black America
Who's Who In Social Services

Bill of Rights (First Ten Amendments to the United States Constitution)

Original Ten Amendments: The Bill of Rights

Passed by Congress September 25, 1789.
Ratified December 15, 1791.

Amendment I

Freedoms, Petitions, Assembly

Congress shall make no law respecting an establishment of religion, or prohibiting the free exercise thereof; or abridging the freedom of speech, or of the press, or the right of the people peaceably to assemble, and to petition the Government for a redress of grievances.

Amendment II

Right to bear arms

A well regulated Militia, being necessary to the security of a free State, the right of the people to keep and bear Arms, shall not be infringed.

Amendment III

Quartering of soldiers

No Soldier shall, in time of peace be quartered in any house, without the consent of the Owner, nor in time of war, but in a manner to be prescribed by law.

Amendment IV

Search and arrest

The right of the people to be secure in their persons, houses, papers, and effects, against unreasonable searches and seizures, shall not be violated, and no Warrants shall issue, but upon probable cause, supported by Oath or affirmation, and particularly describing the place to be searched, and the persons or things to be seized.

Amendment V

Rights in criminal cases

No person shall be held to answer for a capital, or otherwise infamous crime, unless on a presentment or indictment of a Grand Jury, except in cases arising in the land or naval forces, or in the Militia, when in actual service in time of War or public danger; nor shall any person be subject for the same offence to be twice put in jeopardy of life or limb, nor shall be compelled in any criminal case to be a witness against himself, nor be deprived of life, liberty, or property, without due process of law; nor shall private property be taken for public use, without just compensation.

Amendment VI

Right to a fair trial

In all criminal prosecutions, the accused shall enjoy the right to a speedy and public trial, by an impartial jury of the State and district wherein the crime shall have been committed; which district shall have been previously ascertained by law, and to be informed of the nature and cause of the accusation; to be confronted with the witnesses against him; to have compulsory process for obtaining witnesses in his favor, and to have the assistance of counsel for his defence.

Amendment VII

Rights in civil cases

In Suits at common law, where the value in controversy shall exceed twenty dollars, the right of trial by jury shall be preserved, and no fact tried by a jury shall be otherwise re-examined in any Court of the United States, than according to the rules of the common law.

Amendment VIII

Bail, fines, punishment

Excessive bail shall not be required, nor excessive fines imposed, nor cruel and unusual punishments inflicted.

Amendment IX

Rights retained by the People

The enumeration in the Constitution of certain rights shall not be construed to deny or disparage others retained by the people.

Amendment X

States' rights

The powers not delegated to the United States by the Constitution, nor prohibited by it to the States, are reserved to the States respectively, or to the people.

United States of America
The Declaration of Independence

IN CONGRESS, July 4, 1776.

The unanimous Declaration of the thirteen united States of America,

When in the Course of human events, it becomes necessary for one people to dissolve the political bands which have connected them with another, and to assume among the powers of the earth, the separate and equal station to which the Laws of Nature and of Nature's God entitle them, a decent respect to the opinions of mankind requires that they should declare the causes which impel them to the separation.

We hold these truths to be self-evident, that all men are created equal, that they are endowed by their Creator with certain unalienable Rights, that among these are Life, Liberty and the pursuit of Happiness.--That to secure these rights, Governments are instituted among Men, deriving their just powers from the consent of the governed, --That whenever any Form of Government becomes destructive of these ends, it is the Right of the People to alter or to abolish it, and to institute new Government, laying its foundation on such principles and organizing its powers in such form, as to them shall seem most likely to effect their Safety and Happiness. Prudence, indeed, will dictate that Governments long established should not be changed for light and transient causes; and accordingly all experience hath shewn, that mankind are more disposed to suffer, while evils are sufferable, than to right themselves by abolishing the forms to which they are accustomed. But when a long train of abuses and usurpations, pursuing invariably the same Object evinces a design to reduce them under absolute Despotism, it is their right, it is their duty, to throw off such Government, and to provide new Guards for their future security.--Such has been the patient sufferance of these Colonies; and such is now the necessity which constrains them to alter their former Systems of Government. The history of the present King of Great Britain is a history of repeated injuries and usurpations, all having in direct object the establishment of an absolute Tyranny over these States. To prove this, let Facts be submitted to a candid world.

He has refused his Assent to Laws, the most wholesome and necessary for the public good.

He has forbidden his Governors to pass Laws of immediate and pressing importance, unless suspended in their operation till his Assent should be obtained; and when so suspended, he has utterly neglected to attend to them.

He has refused to pass other Laws for the accommodation of large districts of people, unless those people would relinquish the right of Representation in the Legislature, a right inestimable to them and formidable to tyrants only.

He has called together legislative bodies at places unusual, uncomfortable, and distant from the depository of their public Records, for the sole purpose of fatiguing them into compliance with his measures.

He has dissolved Representative Houses repeatedly, for opposing with manly firmness his invasions on the rights of the people.

He has refused for a long time, after such dissolutions, to cause others to be elected; whereby the Legislative powers, incapable of Annihilation, have returned to the People at large for their exercise; the State remaining in the mean time exposed to all the dangers of invasion from without, and convulsions within.

He has endeavored to prevent the population of these States; for that purpose obstructing the Laws for Naturalization of Foreigners; refusing to pass others to encourage their migrations hither, and raising the conditions of new Appropriations of Lands.

He has obstructed the Administration of Justice, by refusing his Assent to Laws for establishing Judiciary powers.

He has made Judges dependent on his Will alone, for the tenure of their offices, and the amount and payment of their salaries.

He has erected a multitude of New Offices, and sent hither swarms of Officers to harrass our people, and eat out their substance.

He has kept among us, in times of peace, Standing Armies without the Consent of our legislatures.

He has affected to render the Military independent of and superior to the Civil power.

He has combined with others to subject us to a jurisdiction foreign to our constitution, and unacknowledged by our laws; giving his Assent to their Acts of pretended Legislation:

For Quartering large bodies of armed troops among us:

For protecting them, by a mock Trial, from punishment for any Murders which they should commit on the Inhabitants of these States:

For cutting off our Trade with all parts of the world:

For imposing Taxes on us without our Consent:

For depriving us in many cases, of the benefits of Trial by Jury:

For transporting us beyond Seas to be tried for pretended offences

For abolishing the free System of English Laws in a neighbouring Province, establishing therein an Arbitrary government, and enlarging its Boundaries so as to render it at once an example and fit instrument for introducing the same absolute rule into these Colonies:

For taking away our Charters, abolishing our most valuable Laws, and altering fundamentally the Forms of our Governments:

For suspending our own Legislatures, and declaring themselves invested with power to legislate for us in all cases whatsoever.

He has abdicated Government here, by declaring us out of his Protection and waging War against us.

He has plundered our seas, ravaged our Coasts, burnt our towns, and destroyed the lives of our people.

He is at this time transporting large Armies of foreign Mercenaries to compleat the works of death, desolation and tyranny, already begun with circumstances of Cruelty & perfidy scarcely paralleled in the most barbarous ages, and totally unworthy the Head of a civilized nation.

He has constrained our fellow Citizens taken Captive on the high Seas to bear Arms against their Country, to become the executioners of their friends and Brethren, or to fall themselves by their Hands.

He has excited domestic insurrections amongst us, and has endeavoured to bring on the inhabitants of our frontiers, the merciless Indian Savages, whose known rule of warfare, is an undistinguished destruction of all ages, sexes and conditions.

In every stage of these Oppressions We have Petitioned for Redress in the most humble terms: Our repeated Petitions have been answered only by repeated injury. A Prince whose character is thus marked by every act which may define a Tyrant, is unfit to be the ruler of a free people.

Nor have We been wanting in attentions to our Brittish brethren. We have warned them from time to time of attempts by their legislature to extend an unwarrantable jurisdiction over us. We have reminded them of the circumstances of our emigration and settlement here. We have appealed to their native justice and magnanimity, and we have conjured them by the ties of our common kindred to disavow these usurpations, which, would inevitably interrupt our connections and correspondence. They too have been deaf to the voice of justice and of consanguinity. We must, therefore, acquiesce in the necessity, which denounces our Separation, and hold them, as we hold the rest of mankind, Enemies in War, in Peace Friends.

We, therefore, the Representatives of the united States of America, in General Congress, Assembled, appealing to the Supreme Judge of the world for the rectitude of our intentions, do, in the Name, and by Authority of the good People of these Colonies, solemnly publish and declare, That these United Colonies are, and of Right ought to be Free and Independent States; that they are Absolved from all Allegiance to the British Crown, and that all political connection between them and the State of Great Britain, is and ought to be totally dissolved; and that as Free and Independent States, they have full Power to levy War, conclude Peace, contract Alliances, establish Commerce, and to do all other Acts and Things which Independent States may of right do. And for the support of this Declaration, with a firm reliance on the protection of divine Providence, we mutually pledge to each other our Lives, our Fortunes and our sacred Honor.

United Nations
New York, NY
Universal Declaration of Human Rights

On December 10, 1948 the General Assembly of the United Nations adopted and proclaimed the Universal Declaration of Human Rights the full text of which appears in the following pages. Following this historic act the Assembly called upon all Member countries to publicize the text of the Declaration and "to cause it to be disseminated, displayed, read and expounded principally in schools and other educational institutions, without distinction based on the political status of countries or territories."

PREAMBLE

Whereas recognition of the inherent dignity and of the equal and inalienable rights of all members of the human family is the foundation of freedom, justice and peace in the world,

Whereas disregard and contempt for human rights have resulted in barbarous acts which have outraged the conscience of mankind, and the advent of a world in which human beings shall enjoy freedom of speech and belief and freedom from fear and want has been proclaimed as the highest aspiration of the commonpeople,

Whereas it is essential, if man is not to be compelled to have recourse, as a last resort, to rebellion against tyranny and oppression, that human rights should be protected by the rule of law,

Whereas it is essential to promote the development of friendly relations between nations,

Whereas the peoples of the United Nations have in the Charter reaffirmed their faith in fundamental human rights, in the dignity and worth of the human person and in the equal rights of men and women and have determined to promote social progress and better standards of life in larger freedom,

Whereas Member States have pledged themselves to achieve, in co-operation with the United Nations, the promotion of universal respect for and observance of human rights and fundamental freedoms,

Whereas a common understanding of these rights and freedoms is of the greatest importance for the full realization of this pledge,

Now, Therefore,

THE GENERAL ASSEMBLY

proclaims

THIS UNIVERSAL DECLARATION OF HUMAN RIGHTS as a common standard of achievement for all peoples and all nations, to the end that every individual and every organ of society, keeping this Declaration constantly in mind, shall strive by teaching and education to promote respect for these rights and freedoms and by progressive measures, national and international, to secure their universal and effective recognition and observance, both among the peoples of Member States themselves and among the peoples of territories under their jurisdiction.

Article 1.

All human beings are born free and equal in dignity and rights. They are endowed with reason and conscience and should act towards one another in a spirit of brotherhood.

Article 2.

Everyone is entitled to all the rights and freedoms set forth in this Declaration, without distinction of any kind, such as race, colour, sex, language, religion, political or other opinion, national or social origin, property, birth or other status. Furthermore, no distinction shall be made on the basis of the political, jurisdictional or international status of the country or territory to which a person belongs, whether it be independent, trust, non-self-governing or under any other limitation of sovereignty.

Article 3.

Everyone has the right to life, liberty and security of person.

Article 4.

No one shall be held in slavery or servitude; slavery and the slave trade shall be prohibited in all their forms.

Article 5.

No one shall be subjected to torture or to cruel, inhuman or degrading treatment or punishment.

Article 6.

Everyone has the right to recognition everywhere as a person before the law.

Article 7.

All are equal before the law and are entitled without any discrimination to equal protection of the law. All are entitled to equal protection against any discrimination in violation of this Declaration and against any incitement to such discrimination.

Article 8.

Everyone has the right to an effective remedy by the competent national tribunals for acts violating the fundamental rights granted him by the constitution or by law.

Article 9.

No one shall be subjected to arbitrary arrest, detention or exile.

Article 10.

Everyone is entitled in full equality to a fair and public hearing by an independent and impartial tribunal, in the determination of his rights and obligations and of any criminal charge against him.

Article 11.

(1) Everyone charged with a penal offence has the right to be presumed innocent until proved guilty according to law in a public trial at which he has had all the guarantees necessary for his defence.

(2) No one shall be held guilty of any penal offence on account of any act or omission which did not constitute a penal offence, under national or international law, at the time when it was committed Nor shall a heavier penalty be imposed than the one that was applicable at the time the penal offence was committed.

Article 12.

No one shall be subjected to arbitrary interference with his privacy, family, home or correspondence, nor to attacks upon his honour and reputation Everyone has the right to the protection of the law against such interference or attacks.

Article 13.

(1) Everyone has the right to freedom of movement and residence within the borders of each state.

(2) Everyone has the right to leave any country, including his own, and to return to his country.

Article 14.

(1) Everyone has the right to seek and to enjoy in other countries asylum from persecution.

(2) This right may not be invoked in the case of prosecutions genuinely arising from non-political crimes or from acts contrary to the purposes and principles of the United Nations.

Article 15.

(1) Everyone has the right to a nationality.

(2) No one shall be arbitrarily deprived of his nationality nor denied the right to change his nationality.

Article 16.

(1) Men and women of full age, without any limitation due to race, nationality or religion, have the right to marry and to found a family. They are entitled to equal rights as to marriage, during marriage and at its dissolution.

(2) Marriage shall be entered into only with the free and full consent of the intending spouses.

(3) The family is the natural and fundamental group unit of society and is entitled to protection by society and the State.

Article 17.

(1) Everyone has the right to own property alone as well as in association with others.

(2) No one shall be arbitrarily deprived of his property.

Article 18.

Everyone has the right to freedom of thought, conscience and religion; this right includes freedom to change his religion or belief, and freedom, either alone or in community with others and in public or private, to manifest his religion or belief in teaching, practice, worship and observance.

Article 19.

Everyone has the right to freedom of opinion and expression; this right includes freedom to hold opinions without interference and to seek, receive and impart information and ideas through any media and regardless of frontiers.

Article 20.

(1) Everyone has the right to freedom of peaceful assembly and association.

(2) No one may be compelled to belong to an association.

Article 21.

(1) Everyone has the right to take part in the government of his country, directly or through freely chosen representatives.

(2) Everyone has the right to equal access to public service in his country.

(3) The will of the people shall be the basis of the authority of government; this shall be expressed in periodic and genuine elections which shall be by universal and equal suffrage and shall be held by secret vote or by equivalent free voting procedures.

Article 22.

Everyone, as a member of society, has the right to social security and is entitled to realization, through national effort and international co-operation and in accordance with the organization and resources of each

State, of the economic, social and cultural rights indispensable for his dignity and the free development of his personality.

Article 23.

(1) Everyone has the right to work, to free choice of employment, to just and favourable conditions of work and to protection against unemployment.

(2) Everyone, without any discrimination, has the right to equal pay for equal work.

(3) Everyone who works has the right to just and favourable remuneration ensuring for himself and his family an existence worthy of human dignity, and supplemented, if necessary, by other means of social protection.

(4) Everyone has the right to form and to join trade unions for the protection of his interests.

Article 24.

Everyone has the right to rest and leisure, including reasonable limitation of working hours and periodic holidays with pay.

Article 25.

(1) Everyone has the right to a standard of living adequate for the health and well-being of himself and of his family, including food, clothing, housing and medical care and necessary social services, and the right to security in the event of unemployment, sickness, disability, widowhood, old age or other lack of livelihood in circumstances beyond his control.

(2) Motherhood and childhood are entitled to special care and assistance. All children, whether born in or out of wedlock, shall enjoy the same social protection.

Article 26.

(1) Everyone has the right to education. Education shall be free, at least in the elementary and fundamental stages. Elementary education shall be compulsory. Technical and professional education shall be made generally available and higher education shall be equally accessible to all on the basis of merit.

(2) Education shall be directed to the full development of the human personality and to the strengthening of respect for human rights and fundamental freedoms. It shall promote understanding, tolerance and friendship among all nations, racial or religious groups, and shall further the activities of the United Nations for the maintenance of peace.

(3) Parents have a prior right to choose the kind of education that shall be given to their children.

Article 27.

(1) Everyone has the right freely to participate in the cultural life of the community, to enjoy the arts and to share in scientific advancement and its benefits.

(2) Everyone has the right to the protection of the moral and material interests resulting from any scientific, literary or artistic production of which he is the author.

Article 28.

Everyone is entitled to a social and international order in which the rights and freedoms set forth in this Declaration can be fully realized.

Article 29.

(1) Everyone has duties to the community in which alone the free and full development of his personality is possible.

(2) In the exercise of his rights and freedoms, everyone shall be subject only to such limitations as are determined by law solely for the purpose of securing due recognition and respect for the rights and freedoms of others and of meeting the just requirements of morality, public order and the general welfare in a democratic society.

(3) These rights and freedoms may in no case be exercised contrary to the purposes and principles of the United Nations.

Article 30.

Nothing in this Declaration may be interpreted as implying for any State, group or person any right to engage in any activity or to perform any act aimed at the destruction of any of the rights and freedoms set forth herein.

CPSIA information can be obtained at www.ICGtesting.com
Printed in the USA
LVOW10s1421170115

423279LV00006B/10/P